GIVE ME WATER

A history of the River Yealm Regatta

1890 - 2009

Mike Hockaday

Publisher © Mike Hockaday 2010

Printed and bound in 2010 by Bretonside Copy
50-54 Breton Side, Plymouth Devon, England PL4 0AU
Tel: 01752 665254

Layout, design, image manipulation and typeset by Graphic designer Sarah Sweet
Tel: 01752 872828 www.slsweetdesign.blogspot.com

Cover Design Sarah Sweet

ISBN 978-0-9565905-0-3

Contents

Acknowledgements

As time marches on the information for compiling a book such as 'Give Me Water' is made more difficult as information and records become scarce. Around 12 months ago I decided to collect as much information and photographic material as possible on this subject and assemble it into one publication, thus preserving historic material and memories made available by senior members of the community. Hopefully future generations will enjoy this book which has been well supported by regatta followers. Many of the people who contributed have also been keen competitors and passionate supporters of the Yealm regatta over the years.

I have been very fortunate in many people being very generous in lending rare photographic material and giving up their time to talk about regattas and village life over the years.

My thanks are expressed to the following people: The Stitson family of Vera, Wendy, Pete and Jane, Tony Tubb, Peter Leonard, Ron and Rosemary Furzeland, Dave and Lorraine Walker, Mike and Jill Leonard-Williams, Tommy Taylor, Rodney and Jane Carter, Emma Cawse, Paul and Margaret Francombe, Jan Dowling, Phil and Kairen Carter, Barbara and Warwick Hemming, Kirsten Monsen, Roger Aggett, Mike Parsons, Peter Modley, Den Shepherd, Pat Groome, Maurice Farleigh, John Shepherd, Peter Hicks, Sasha James, Maxine Sherrell, Chris George, John Roach, Claire Cassidy, Kate Watkinson, Howard Swift for providing drawing of 'Shamrock', Andrew Matthews and James Manners for proof reading, Paul Bullen for providing front and back cover photo, Christine Thery for letting me use the many fine photographs she took of the regattas in the 1970s, South Hams Newspapers and the Western Morning News.

John, Jack and Harry Hockaday who might as well build a museum for all the archive material they have collected on the villages of Newton and Noss over the years. A big thank you to Sarah Sweet who has spent countless hours applying her artistic expertise in designing and formatting the book. Also her invaluable photo re-touching skills applied to many older photographs, ensuring that when reproduced they are of a high standard. Special thank you to Debbie Hemming who has patiently sat with me for many hours, sifting through photographs and text and applying her editing skills, along with much advice on structure and layout of the book.

Mike Hockaday

Yealm Crabber
Shamrock
Built 1898
Showing spritsail rig
Circa 1920
Loa 21 ft 6in   Beam 6ft 6in

Introduction

"GIVE ME WATER!"

Those three words have been shouted across to rival boats in many a regatta on the River Yealm for more than a hundred years. Whilst this request is intended to create space between boats as they race, it does not always receive the attention it is meant to. Harry Hockaday (*snr*), Yealm lifeboat coxswain from 1898 to 1927, used to reply to this request on a regular basis with a baler full of water from the bilges of the Crabber he was coxing. Apparently, his antics of giving rival coxes a good soaking were not well received. I expect he hoped the distraction he created might give him a slight edge in the 'Greyback Race', by all accounts fiercely contested in those pre-second world war years.

Since those early regattas, I don't suppose a year has gone by without some controversy occurring in the Yealm regatta. Even today, coxes are often to be heard shouting for water, in the hope of giving their crew a slight advantage over their rivals. Some competitors do not yield easily, even when oars are clashing and the shouts take on a more colourful language. It then takes a very strict umpire on the megaphone to warn offending competitors to give water or face disqualification.

The Yealm regatta seems to bring out more passion in people than any other village event I can think of. Over the years, I recall many heated arguments between competitors, Committee members, and spectators. On the other hand, I also remember the regatta as a time when people thoroughly enjoy themselves, either competing or enjoying light refreshments on the spectator boats. When the sun is shining, young people, and occasionally older ones, jump out of their boats to cool off. All these things add up to create the atmosphere of the regatta - a colourful scene, mixed with quite a number of colourful characters.

I hope this book brings together the scenes of years gone by, and describes the people and events of the Yealm regatta that has taken place for well over 100 years in this unique location.

1890 - 1939
Early Regattas and Yealm Crabbers

Early regattas at 'The Pool'

The earliest mention I have found of a Yealm regatta dates from 1880s in Maurice Barings' book 'The Puppet Show of Memory' (Maurice Baring, 2001). Maurice was the son of Edward Baring who, as well as being a Director of the Bank of England and senior partner at Baring Bros., was also the 1st Baron Revelstoke (the parish of Revelstoke later became the parish of Noss Mayo). In his book, Maurice describes his childhood memories on the Membland Estate during the latter part of the 19th century, recalling:

> "Another source of joy in Membland life was the yacht, the Waterwitch, which in the summer months used to sail as soon as the Cowes Regatta was over, down to the Yealm River. The Waterwitch was a schooner of 150 tons; it had one large cabin where one had one's meals, my mother's cabin aft, a cabin for my father, and three spare cabins. The name of the first captain was Goomes, but he was afterwards replaced by Bletchington. Goomes was employed later by the German Emperor. He had a knack of always getting into rows during races, and even on other occasions. One day there was a regatta going on on the Yealm River; the gig of the Waterwitch was to race the gig of another yacht. They had to go round a buoy. For some reason, I was in the Waterwitch's gig when the race started, sitting in the stern next to Goomes, who was steering. All went well at first, but when the boats were going round the buoy they fouled, and Goomes and the skipper of the rival gig were soon engaged in a hand-to-hand combat, and beating each other hard with the steering-lines. My father and the rest of the family were watching the race on board the yacht. I think I was about six or seven. My father shouted at the top of his voice, "Come back, come back," but to no avail, as Goomes and the other skipper were fighting like two dogs, and the boats were almost capsizing. I think Goomes won the fight and the race. I remember enjoying it all heartily, but not so my father on board the yacht."

Although it is likely that rowing and sailing races were going on in the early and mid 19th century, records of the early regattas are a bit sketchy. Nevertheless, some photos and documents have survived and other information has been handed down through families. There is evidence that a variety of races were held, including single, pair oared and shovel races. Sailing races were also part of the programme, and these included the working Crabbing boats and Gentlemen's dayboats.

C.1890 Edward Baring's Schooner the 'Waterwitch' lying on her mooring in The Pool.

Back in pre-World War I (WWI) days, there were two separate regattas - the Bridgend regatta and the Yealm regatta. Unfortunately, I have been unable to find any official records of the Bridgend regatta, except that it finished in 1914 at the outbreak of WWI. However, the Yealm regatta (also referred to in some documents of the time as the Newton Ferrers regatta), which was held in The Pool just off the Yealm Hotel, gained in popularity both before and after WWI.

In 1922, Archie Nelder, a Wembury farmer, was a key driving force in starting the Wembury regatta, which also took place in The Pool, and in the Kitley branch of the river. At that time a number of individuals were building their own boats to compete in the regattas. It must have been a bit like grand prix racing. As each season arrived, sleeker and faster designs appeared on the river giving, of course, some competitors a distinct advantage in the racing. No doubt after racing had finished arguments would continue over who had the fastest boat on the river.

Wembury regattas normally finished up with a spectacular fireworks display organised by the Nelder family and launched from Warren Point opposite the Yealm Hotel. There was no shortage of fireworks as Mrs Nelder (*nee* Brock) was associated with the famous Brocks firework company.

The pictures over the following pages illustrate that the regattas of this period were very grand occasions, with hundreds of spectators dressed in their finery, arriving from Plymouth on paddle steamers such as the 'Princess Royal'.

5

C.1910 spectators gathering to watch the Yealm regatta at The Pool.

C.1910 Yealm regatta in full swing in The Pool, with the houseboat 'Lamorna' and one of the local Herring Drifters in the foreground, and the 'Princess Royal' paddle steamer in the background.

C.1910 Yealm sailing regatta at the mouth of the river showing Yealm Crabbers in the foreground with their spritsail rigs, because of light conditions they are sporting topsails.

C.1910 Yealm sailing regatta at the mouth of the river, showing Gentlemen's dayboats in the foreground with their Gunter and Gaff rigs.

C.1910 View of unknown rowers posing for the camera at Cellars Beach at the mouth of the river.

C.1910 the paddle steamer 'Princess Royal' heading up past Misery Point loaded with passengers enjoying a day out on the Yealm.

C.1920 regatta day at The Pool, spectators taking up position and flying their Union Jacks.

C.1920 view of the 'Kitley Belle' moored between Newton Brook and Noss Creek. She was hired on a regular basis by the regatta Committee for ferrying spectators from Steer Point railway station to the regatta.

C.1919 start of the running race outside the Tilly Institute in Noss Mayo.
Runners identified are no2 Charlie Axworthy and no17 Phil Hockaday.
Perhaps this race was the regatta Mini Marathon of the time.

Winner of the running race, Charlie Axworthy approaching the finish line being
cheered on enthusiastically by Harry Hockaday (snr) standing in front of the
bicycle wheel to the left.

1919-1920 Yealm United Football Club. Back row from left to right E. Gill, C. Lake, P. Hockaday, E. Blackmore, F. Lake, W. Staplehurst. Second row V. Hodge, F. Roseveare, A. Roach, S. Roach, J. Hisbent, H. Squire, F. Land. Third row N. Bunker, E. Richards, E. Shepherd, N. Wyatt, G. Mears, G. Bunker, J. Tope, A. Tope, F. Wyatt. Front Row: H. Kingcome, J. Axworthy, J. Hodge, W. Tope, R. Kingcome.

C.1930 Yealm United Football Club. People recognized, back row from left to right S. Shepherd, ?, C. Lake, ?, A. Roach, J. Tope, ?, ?, R. Baker, J. Hisbent, H. Sims. Middle Row G. Hockaday, ?, ?, B. Crook, ?, ?, L. Roach far right, Front Row ?, O. Shepherd, S. Foster, S. Squires, ?, W. Hockaday ?.

The early regattas were always keenly supported by the local press. The following extracts are from the South Devon Times, 26th August 1926.

"The River Yealm regatta took place on Saturday in fair weather, the grey clouds and drizzly rain which threatened earlier events passed over, and brilliant sunshine cheered the rest of the proceedings the races were keenly contested and their were many close finishes. The band of the 5th (P of W Battalion) Devonshire regiment discoarsed music.

Some of the rowing results are as follows:
Pair-oared race for ladies (with Cox) 1st place is Miss B. Tope, 2nd place Miss C. Algate, 3rd place Miss K. Selwood.

Yealm Challenge Cup race for Men. Single sculls in inrigged boats 14ft and under, 4ft 6in beam, bonafide punts as used on the Yealm only eligible and to be 3/8in (minimum plank thickness). 1st place V. Hodge, 2nd place E. Foster, A. Nelder (dead heat).

Ladies Challenge Cup race (same rules apply) 1st place Miss B. Tope, 2nd place Miss N. Nelder, 3rd place Miss K. Selwood.

Greyback race in Yealm Crabbers boats 18ft and over, 4 oars and coxswain 1st place G. Hockaday, 2nd place R. Hockaday, 3rd place C. Tope.

The handicap motorboat race, Single Cylinder engines only. 1st place Mr J. Truran, 2nd place Mr. J. Dyer, 3rd place Major D. Todd.

The Swimming races held yesterday evening in connection with the Yealm regatta created some good sport. The two challenge cup races, one for men and the other for ladies aroused a great deal of interest, J. Dyer won the mens cup although H. Goodman who finished 2nd, beat him in the open race over 300yds - the same distance. Miss Nora Hereford who is only 13 years of age was the outstanding girl swimmer, winning two events in addition to the Yealm Challenge cup, presented by Col. Craven-Hoyle.

Some of the swimming results are as follows:
Ladies Yealm challenge cup 150yds. 1st place N. Hereford, 2nd place S. Williams, 3rd place M. Hodge.

Yealm Challenge cup for men 300yds. 1st place J. Dyer, 2nd place H. Goodman, 3rd place R. Baker.

<u>Ladies race (open)150yds.</u> 1st place J. Tilly, 2nd place N. Hereford, 3rd place A. Libby.

<u>Mens race (open).</u> 1st place H. Goodman, 2nd place J. Dyer, 3rd place E. Dyer.

The Water Carnival

The regatta terminated in a water carnival on Saturday when the chief spectacle dealt with events on the pre-historic Yealm. At 5.30pm there was a discovery of the Yealm by the Newton Nibelungs and the Noss Ghazigazooks. Gaily decorated boats, in all kinds of colour schemes were gliding along majestically and from a gramophone in a punt somewhere under the overhanging foliage on the farther bank of the river, came the strains of popular dance music. Suddenly a loud report rent the air, and the two savage tribes met in their war canoes. After a prolonged struggle, during which many of the warriors were precipitated into the chilly waters, the Nibelungs proved themselves superior in Naval strategy. Tired by their exertions the tribesmen declared a truce and settled down with the civilized population to witness the scheduled firework display which presented a kaleidoscopic spectacle".

(South Devon Times, 26th August 1926)

1925 Jim Dyer, champion swimmer, worked on the River Yealm Oyster beds for many years.

C.1920 view from Wembury to Ferry Cottage on regatta day.

C.1910 four Yealm Crabbers sailing out to the mouth of the Yealm to compete in the sailing regatta.

C.1910 a large trading vessel moored off Noss Creek.

C.1920 'Kitley Belle' lying along side Popes Quay with the Globe Inn in the background.

C.1910 Scene directly below Ferry Cottage, Noss Mayo. Was there gig racing on the river Yealm at this time?

C.1920 Yealm regatta at The Pool, view looking towards the lifeboat house and the Yealm Hotel.

C.1910 Yealm regatta at The Pool, showing ladies dressed in all their finery.

C.1920 Yealm regatta at The Pool, showing in the foreground a shovel race crew and in the background the 'Kitley Belle' at Wide Slip.

The oldest regatta trophy still competed for is the 'Yealm Hotel Cup', which was presented for the 1911 Yealm regatta by *Messrs.* Kingcome and Tenney, owners of the Yealm Hotel at the time. They stipulated that the race for this cup was to be rowed in Yealm Crabbers, the boats were to represent the two villages of Noss Mayo and Newton Ferrers, and the oarsmen were to be men who worked on the land, probably to encourage those not used to being on the water to take part. At some stage, this became known as the 'Greyback' race. Den Shepherd (born 1922), resi-  dent of Noss Mayo, recalls that the term Greyback derives from the colour of the land workers skin. In those days large quantities of lime were spread on the fields manually, and when mixed with the soil it created clouds of dust which covered the workers, giving them a greyish appearance. After a few years, Kingcome and Tenney's original stipulations seemed to fall by the wayside. Fishermen and other people who worked on the water also began to compete in this race. However, even to this day many still refer to the Men's Crabbing boat race as the Greyback race.

C.1910 Crabber 'Snowdrop' (PH158) owned by George Foster in Noss Creek.
Snowdrop was regularly rowed in the Greyback race up until 1939.

C.1920 typical regatta day at The Pool. (It is believed that the gig in the centre of this photo was owned by the Jago family from Cawsands).

C.1920 typical regatta day at The Pool.

Early 1920s regatta day at The Pool, showing the houseboat 'Chonita' in position and dressed overall.

C.1920 view of the 'Kitley Belle' heading up the Kitley branch of the river to Steer Point. Could she be collecting spectators travelling out on the train from Plymouth?

C.1920 photo showing a Skiff just off the Yealm Hotel pier - perhaps this is the one that Ernest Hodge came to grief in!

Another hotly competed race during the 1900 to 1920s period was the Skiff race. A number of these Skiffs were built to high racing specifications by local Noss craftsmen Tom Algate, Elliott Hodge, and Lando Leonard. In one particular race, Ernest Hodge was leading in a Skiff called the 'Nona', built by his brother Elliott, when suddenly the thwart support on which he was sitting failed and his posterior broke through the thin planking and 1 inch square keel in the bottom of the boat. He glided to a gentle halt as the other competitors raced past.

Competition was very keen in those early years. My grandfather, Bill Hockaday (1909-2007), recalled that the Crabber crews from Newton and Noss would go to great lengths to prepare their boats for the Greyback race each year. To make them lighter, all Crabbers were taken out of the water to dry - the Newton Crabbers at 'The Brook' and the Noss Crabbers at 'Noss Creek'. Bill also remembered that the young lads in the villages were put to work applying black lead to the undersides of the boats, which provided a clean, smooth surface.

Different courses for the Greyback race were tried over the years. As the race became more closely contested, a decision was made to try running the race from the mouth of the Yealm up Newton Creek, to a mark at Bridgend, then back to finish off Noss Creek. The idea was that the Crabbers would spread out over the distance, avoiding very controversial clashes while rounding the buoys, which often lead to heated arguments.

Besides the sailing and rowing races, the early Wembury regatta had organized fast speed-boat races that took place up the Kitley branch of the River Yealm. These boats were between 14ft and 16ft long, mostly powered by 32hp American Elto quad motors, and were capable of speeds close to 35kn. In those days, there were very few boats moored up the Kitley, which left a bit of room for error! For the 1930 Wembury regatta speed boat race, aircraftsman T. E. Lawrence, better known as Lawrence of Arabia, arrived in his boat, the 'Biscuit', and was competing against other RAF personnel and Mr Skentelbery, a local boat builder who was racing a small hydro plane called 'Nippy III'. After the racing Lawrence returned to his base at Mountbatten by road, while the other RAF competitors decided to return in their speed boats. Due to poor weather they got into difficulties off the Mewstone, and the Plymouth lifeboat was called out to assist. The following is an extract about this rescue from the book 'Wreck and rescue on the coast of Devon'. (Grahame Farr, 1968)

"The rescue from the Royal Air Force boats in 1930 was a case where service families returning from a day in the Yealm, where they had attended Wembury regatta, were suddenly enveloped in fog and had to anchor in the vicinity of the Mewstone. Fortunately the wind and sea did not increase, and after a lengthy search they were found all well but cold and wet at 4.o'clock in the morning."

C.1930 T. E. Lawrence racing in his speed boat the 'Biscuit'.

C.1930 view of the course where T. E. Lawrence would have raced his speed boat 'Biscuit' showing how clear of moored boats the Kitley branch of the river was at this time.

The Yearm Crabbers

At this point, I thought it would be worthwhile to write some more detail about the Yealm Crabbers, particularly their role as working boats, and of course there involvement in the Yealm regattas.

At its height around 1900, the local Yealm fishing fleet comprised approximately 30 Crabbers and 5 Herring Drifters and Lining boats. Crabbers were anything between 18ft and 22ft long, and approximately 6ft 10in in the beam. They were sturdily constructed of larch planking on steamed oak timbers, most of which were cut locally on the Kitley and Puslinch Estates. These boats were provided with a spritsail rig, which was favoured by the fishermen as it was quick to lower at sea once the fishing grounds had been reached. It must have been a hard and risky way to make a living, battling under sail and oar against wind and tide in these small open boats.

C.1910 view of Noss Creek featuring the Crabbers 'Thistle' (PH272)
owned by Edgar Foster, and 'Snowdrop' (PH158) owned
by George Foster.

A normal season for the Crabbers started on Valentine's Day, and ended around Christmas. Most of the boats worked about 40 crab pots from the mouth of the River Erme (in Bigbury Bay), out to the West Rutts and in to the Mewstone (in Wembury Bay). That was considered to be 'Yealmer' territory. Fishermen from Hope Cove, Salcombe and Plymouth learned to steer clear of this ground, as it was typical for outsiders' pots to be hauled and catches removed. There was an abundance of shell fish to be caught in those days, and it was not unusual to catch two or three crabs per pot. Despite this, prices at market were not always good, and making a decent living was a precarious business.

23

Then of course the hazards of life at sea had to be dealt with. One particularly tragic incident occurred on the 11th April 1898, when five Crabbers were out fishing in Bigbury Bay. The wind started to freshen rapidly from the south west, making it very hard for them to return to the Yealm. Three Crabbers made it safely back to harbour as the conditions worsened. Realising that their fellow fishermen were overdue, the alarm was raised, and the Yealm lifeboat, 'Daring', with 10 oarsmen and cox, William Hockaday (*snr*), was launched. After eventually clearing the mouth of the Yealm in breaking seas and gale-force winds, the crew found it impossible to make an extensive search for the missing men. In the meantime, a crowd of about 100 people had gathered at the Yealm Hotel, adjacent to the lifeboat house, awaiting news of the men, unfortunately their worst fears were confirmed as the 'Daring' appeared in The Pool with its mast light lowered to half mast. The Crabbers lost were the 'Sea-Bird' (PH192) and 'Myrtle'(PH149), and the men lost with them were Dick West (35 yrs) and Alf Banks (42 yrs) in one boat, and Richard Jackson (24 yrs) and George Tucker (47 yrs) in the other. A relief fund was set up in the villages to help the families of the lost men.

C.1894 river Yealm lifeboat crew. Standing, left to right R. Jackson (one of the men lost in the 1898 Crabber tragedy), B. Lugger, G. Axworthy, L. Hockaday, B. West, C. Jackson, A. Tucker, D. Rowe, B. West (snr), C. Jackson (snr) Seated, left to right G. Hockaday, H. Hockaday, G. Hockaday (snr), W. Hockaday (cox). Most of these men would have competed in the regattas of this period.

Names of Yealm Crabbers and their owners around the turn of the century were 'Fear Not' owned by Joey Adams, 'Emily' owned by Lawrence Williams, 'Minnie' owned by Bob Lugger, 'Freda' owned by Sam Shepherd, 'Coconut' owned by Jack Northcott, 'Finch' owned by Vince Hodge, 'Snowdrop' owned by George Foster, 'Eagle' owned by Harold Sims, 'Thistle' owned by Edgar Foster, 'May Queen' owned by Cecil Foster, 'Emma Jane' owned by Bill Leonard, and 'Shamrock' owned by George Hockaday.

One of the Crabbers I would like to mention at this stage is 'Shamrock' which was built c.1890 in the cellar at the Round House, Noss Mayo, by John Hockaday (1812-1906). Quite a number of Crabbers were built at the Round House, and then gently lowered over the steep bank into the river. Partly due to the rigorous working conditions they were subjected to, most of these boats deteriorated and were broken up by the 1940s. However, 'Shamrock' did survive, she disappeared from the river for many years, but later returned to play a vital role in keeping the regatta going. I'll return to 'Shamrock' later in the book.

C.1890 view of the Round House, Noss Mayo, where many of the early Crabbers were built.

C.1910 view of three Crabbers in Noss Creek, one with its heavy sprit-sail hung out to dry. Note in the background the piles of aggregate on the beach and men at work building Newton Voss.

Some early regatta characters

Many characters were involved in the early regattas. Stanley Eastcott Paige (1883-1963) was a well-known character, and keen supporter of the Yealm regatta. He served on the Committee for many years, and was the official regatta race starter on many occasions throughout the 1920s and 1930s. Stanley was born at Battisborough Cross (2 miles south-east of Noss Mayo), the son of a blacksmith. His early school years were spent down the road at Mothercombe village school. As he was growing up, Stanley decided on a farming career, and used to help at South Battisborough Farm. His grandson, Phil Sherrell, recalls Stanley telling him about working on the farm during the 'Great Blizzard' that began on 9th March 1891. The blizzard was exceptional because it snowed continuously for about 30 hours, and was accompanied by hurricane force easterly winds, which raged for over 24 hours. Between the Dover Straits and the Isles of Scilly over 63 ships and at least 200 lives were lost. After surviving the blizzard, Stanley went on to farm in the Torquay area, before returning to purchase Coombe Farm in Noss Mayo. He settled in well in many aspects of village life, becoming a Parish Councillor and Chairman of the Plympton and District Council, as well as a Justice of the Peace. He was well remembered by the regatta fraternity for his hard work on the Committee, and also for donating, on occasion, a pig for the regatta raffle.

> ### Regatta race starters
>
> *The race starters' job is an awkward one, which requires a person of very firm character to ensure that certain enthusiastic competitors are not advantaged by 'getting a flyer' at the start. These individuals quite happily give up their time, patiently lining up competitors for races, firing off the famous 12-bore starting gun, and skilfully making decisions on close finishes, as quite often they are.*

Cecil Foster (1887-1978) was another village character who was keenly involved in the regatta. He was one of nine children, two sisters and seven brothers, and was born in a cottage at the bottom of Newton Hill. When Cecil was 3 years old the family moved to Noss Mayo. As a young man, Cecil started to earn a living from fishing. He worked for many years in his Crabber, 'The May Queen', primarily catching crabs and lobsters. At this time, around the turn of the century, fishing was a mainstay for the Yealm communities, with somewhere in the region of 80 men relying on it for their livelihoods.

Cecil was interviewed by Maurice Farleigh in 1976 about his life around the villages, and his memory was very good even at the age of 88. In this interview, Cecil remembered being very much involved in the local regatta, and rowed in the fishermen's race, which was competed for over many years before the Greyback race came into existence. He carried on rowing several years after WWI, and was also a keen competitor in the regatta sailing, when many of the working Crabbers used to participate.

One interesting story recalled by Cecil tells of the lengths his father, Bill Foster, went to in order to keep the village bakery going when Noss and Newton became isolated during the great blizzard in 1891. During this event, the weather conditions were so severe that all routes to the villages were blocked by snow drifts. After several days, the baker in Noss had run out of yeast for baking the bread, and Bill Foster volunteered to walk to Plymouth to get some. He rowed over to Warren Point, on the Wembury shore, then walked along the coast, struggling over hedges and through snow drifts, until he eventually reached Plymouth. Unfortunately, at the yeast depot, he was disappointed to be told that all supplies of yeast were gone, and the only option was to go to the brewery nearby and obtain a jar of 'lees' a waste product of the brewing process, which contained enough yeast for baking bread. Bill did this, but then had the problem of walking the large jar of lees all the way back to Noss. He decided to walk down to the Barbican to try to find skipper Bob Mashford, who owned the trading barge, 'The Brothers', which frequently sailed into the Yealm with goods for the villages. Luckily, Bill found skipper Mashford, who agreed to take the jar of yeast back to Noss the following day, if the weather eased. Bill was invited to sail back with them to the Yealm, but he decided to stay with his brother, who lived up in the town, for a few days probably thinking it would be more comfortable there than the cut off villages of Newton and Noss. I think this story illustrates how isolated the Yealm communities were at this time, and how much they depended on the trading and fishing boats to sustain them. With all these people being involved in working boats, it must have meant that the regattas of this period were very competitive and well supported.

C.1900 the sailing barge 'Phoenix', by all accounts similar to the Mashford owned barge ' The Brothers'. In the background, the pier off the Yealm Hotel and Wembury Warren.

Edgar Foster (1901-1991), a younger brother of Cecil Foster, grew up with boats and fishing in his blood. As a young man, Edgar teamed up with his brother Cecil to carry on the family tradition of making a living from fishing, which both his father and grandfather had pursued throughout their lives. Edgar's boat was the Crabber, 'Thistle', which his father had asked 'Chants' of Salcombe to build, in 1898, for the grand sum of £16. Not only did Edgar work and make a living from the 'Thistle', he rowed in her as one of the Greyback crew, winning on a number of occasions. He remembered first competing in the 1910 regatta as a cox for the under 16's pair oared race, and went on to become a master of the sculling race, which he won for many years.

Rowing and sailing continued to be a part of Edgar's life for many years. He was the last of several generations of fishermen from the Yealm who had to pit their wits, strength and skills against winds and tides to make a living under sail and oar. In total contrast to the modern-day fishermen, who have reliable weather forecasting, powerful diesel engines and state-of-the-art electronic chart plotters and echo sounders at their disposal. Eventually, as the in-shore shell fish stocks gradually declined, Edgar turned to other ways of making a living ashore.

C.1930 Edgar Foster pictured with his wife, Florence, in his Crabber,' Thistle' (PH272), note the spritsail rig. Apparently Edgar said to the passing photographer "I'll put the sails up, it will look more interesting".

Another character closely involved with the regatta at this time was Ralph Garland Hockaday (1895-1965). As well as coxing the Crabbers on many occasions, Ralph was also one of the official race starters during the 1930s and after WWII. As a young man Ralph helped out in the family boat-building business located in Noss Creek. He joined the Devonshire Regiment at the outbreak of WWI, and was sent to India, before being transferred on to Mesopotamia, where he took part in the seige of Kut-el-Amara. After over 5 months the mainly British garrison surrendered to the Turks, and the prisoners faced a forced march of almost 200 miles across the desert, in temperatures often exceeding 100°F. Ralph became very weak due to lack of food and water, and had to be helped along by two of his friends, Mr Sherriff and Mr Smale from Saltash. After this ordeal, all prisoners were examined by Turkish doctors and those able to walk were sent on a further march. Sadly, both men who helped Ralph failed to survive this second march. Ralph was eventually listed as an exchange prisoner, at this point weighing only 5st 6lb. He did not start his return to England until 3 months after the armistice in 1918, sailing from Port Said to Taranto in southern Italy, then on to Calais by train. He was twice mentioned in dispatches and received the military medal for his efforts in the Kut-el-Amara siege. When he eventually arrived home, in 1919, he was very weak and incapable of much manual work for several years. As he recovered, Ralph returned to boatbuilding, and built a 14ft clinker rowing boat named 'Papyrus' for Vince Hodge (*jnr*). During the regatta, Vince went on to win the Yealm Men's Challenge Cup several times in this boat, and it is worth noting that the 'Papyrus' was built for £14, including oars and rowlocks – that wouldn't pay for the leather on a set of oars today!

One other particularly flamboyant character was Leonard Modley. During the late 1930s, Leonard became commanding officer of RAF Bolt Head, where a number of Spitfire and Hurricane fighter planes were stationed. He used to show up at regatta time in his Tiger Moth bi-plane, diving into the valley bombing the crowds with small bags of flour which had long streamer tails attached to them. On one occasion, Clarence Mumford, who was sitting in the front cockpit, was preparing to drop a flour bomb. Instead of falling clear of the plane, it blew back into Leonard's face, temporarily blinding him. Leonard lost control of the plane which went into a steep dive, but he managed to regain control and level off very close to the water. Spectators thought they were being treated to an aerobatics display, and were applauding enthusiastically as the Tiger Moth accelerated up through the valley, not realising that Leonard had almost crashed!

C.1930 river Yealm which Leonard had a birds eye view of.

Another colourful character, and great sporting man, who became involved in the Yealm regatta, was Captain Glynne Percy of Beacon Hill, Newton Ferrers. On one occasion in the 1920s my grandfather, Bill Hockaday, recalled that Captain Glynne Percy was offering tows to Crabber crews from the pool to the mouth of the river. My great-grandfather, Harry, went to join the tow but was refused. I guess Captain Glynne Percy and Harry did not get on! Harry and his crew, which consisted of his three sons Phil, George and Bill, and Edgar Foster had to row out to the start. Just as they were arriving at the start line and trying to turn around Captain Glynne Percy fired the start gun before they were ready. All ended well though, Harry and his crew caught the others up and won the race.

Another story relating to Captain Glynne Percy, occurred in the 1930s when he had a brush with H.M. Customs and Excise. He owned a large motor vessel called 'The Harpedo' which was moored in The Pool. The story I have been told is that the Harpedo used to frequent the French coast, where brandy and other contraband were taken onboard. On return to the Yealm the contraband was then transferred to Captain Glynne Percy's garden where it was buried. The Customs Officials got wind of this smuggling operation and raided the gardens, apparently digging over the whole garden and removing many boxes of smuggled goods. He was summonsed before Plympton Magistrates and issued with a fine, whereupon he asked the judge if he was happy for the fine to be paid in cash! Captain Glynne Percy was obviously quite a character and by all accounts gave the villagers something to talk about.

The Yealm regatta moves up-river

At a General Meeting held in the Tilly Institute, Noss Mayo, on 8th April 1932, it was decided to amalgamate the Newton Ferrers and Wembury regattas into one under the name of the River Yealm regatta. The two former Committees were re-elected, and the following appointments were duly made: Patroness: Mrs Walker - Wembury House, President: J. Yonge *Esq.* J.P. - Puslinch. Provisional appointments were also made for Chairman: Commander Leycester, Vice Chairman: Mr G. Baker, Treasurer: Mr. Algate, Secretary: Captain C.F. Harrison, Assistant Secretary: A. Nelder *Esq.* At this time, it was decided to move the regatta up river from The Pool to Newton Creek, with the Committee boat stationed off Noss Creek, where it has been ever since.

An amusing memory comes from Den Shepherd, who remembers as a young boy coxing a Newton Youth's Crabber crew c.1934. Den recalls drawing the Newton berth. The boat next to him was a Noss boat and as they were going down creek he was being forced over closer and closer to the Newton shore. No boat outhauls were there in those days, and it got to a stage where Den's crew were heading straight for the doors of Kiln Quay boathouse. By the time Den had persuaded his crew to stop rowing it was too late. The boat had too much way on, and Den and his crew ended up going nowhere as they drifted into the boathouse doors.

Den had been forced off the course by an over enthusiastic Noss cox, to put it politely! Although Den was not in the wrong, he suspected that the Committee lost confidence in his coxing abilities because he remembers being prohibited from coxing for about 5 years after that incident.

I think one reason for competitors in those days being very enthusiastic was the fact that the prize money was very generous. For example, winning first place in the Greyback race was £3, for a Pairs race 15 shillings, and £1 for the adult Challenge Cup races. When you consider that a pint of beer back then was about 1 shilling, and remembering there were 20 shillings to 1 old pound, if you had a good regatta you had a very good pay day.

During the same period, Harry Hockaday who was the second Yealm lifeboat cox and quite a character, was to be seen in his leather sea boots wading out from Newton Brook as the Greyback race was in progress, shaking his fist and shouting at his sons "If you don't win this one, I'll cut yer throats!". They probably had more on their minds when this remark was made as they concentrated on trying to win the race.

C.1935 Greyback race. Perhaps this is the race where the Hockaday brothers were in danger of having their throats cut!

31

1931 preparing for the start of the Men's Pairs race. In the foreground winners Bill and George Hockaday with Lando Leonard and Archie Nelder in the far boat.

1934 start of the Greyback race. Note that five boats were then in race. Winners were Cox. H. Hockaday, Str. G. Hockaday, E. Foster, W. Hockaday and P. Hockaday.

Below are some extracts from the minutes of a 1933 regatta meeting (Chairman was Commander Leycester) held at the Globe Inn (now The Ship) on Friday June 30th, which I think gives a flavour of the events and preparations necessary for the regatta.

"SAILING

It was decided that the two sailing races be started from the usual place at 11.15am respectively. The Service Whalers to be started as before at Mountbatten Breakwater by the RAF and finished between the mark boat stationed at the mouth of the Yealm. The Chairman informed the committee that certain gentlemen owning cruising yachts moored in the Yealm were hoping to arrange a handicap race among themselves, and have asked the committee to loan them the starting guns. Resolution proposed by the Chairman, seconded by Commander May was passed, that the proposed yacht race receive a cup at the discretion of the committee. 'Carried'.

POSTERS

Proposed by Mr Sitters seconded by A.C. Harrison that the Secretary be instructed to procure materials for fifty posters worded as follows: Grand Firework Display to follow regatta on August the 5th 1933 commencing at 9.30pm. Residents are asked to cooperate with the regatta committee on Saturday the 5th August by displaying on their houses and in their gardens, as much bunting and colour as possible.

The secretary was asked to make arrangements for the hire of the 'Kitley Belle' and the 'Pioneer' and to ask for the voluntary attendance of Captain Grieve and his motor boat, which has in previous years been placed at the committee's disposal. Captain Harrison was instructed to arrange hire of two attendant boatmen, one from each village. Messrs A.C. Harrison and L. Sitters agreed to arrange programme depots as was done last year. The committee agreed once more to award a small prize to each boy and girl selling the most programmes.

Mr S.E. Paige generously offered a pig to be raffled in aid of the regatta funds in a similar matter to that donated by Mrs Williamson last year. The committee accepted Mr Paige's offer with pleasure, and expressed their appreciation. The committee then proceeded to appoint the following officers: Sailing: J. Yonge Esq, T. Algate, J. Brooks and Captain Harrison. Rowing Starter: Mr S.E. Paige, Judges: Major Sayers, A.C. Harrison Handicappers: Mr T. Algate, Mr R. Hockaday Timekeeper: Mr E.Foster, Umpires: Major Taylor, Mr Jillard *Jnr.* Competition Stewards: Mr Digges, Commander May, Mr Jillard *Snr.*"

In 1935, 5 new 14ft wooden rowing boats were built by Bill Tope in the old hut part way up Bridgend Hill on the left (which still stands today). These boats were built to even up the Singles and Pairs racing. They served the regatta well and carried on being used up until 1973.

The photograph below of the Tope Brothers after winning the Greyback race in 1939 marks an end to racing in the old working Crabbers. About one month after this, WWII broke out, and this put the Yealm regatta on hold until the end of the war in 1945.

1939 a unique photograph of the Tope Brothers after winning the Greyback race, in the Crabber 'Snowdrop'. Cox. Jack Tope, Str. Bill Tope, Archie, Frank and Gordon Tope.

1945 - 1979
The Introduction of the 'Whaler'

When the regatta recommenced in August 1945, the way of life around the Yealm was changing rapidly. The fishing fleet had all but disappeared fishermen preferring to work from Sutton Harbour in Plymouth, where the landing facilities were good. The barges owned by the Mashford family, which used to bring in coal and other goods for the villages, were no longer required. The 'Kitley Belle', owned by the Hodge family, which used to ferry hundreds of passengers to and fro from Newton and Noss to Steer Point railway station, had been sold off. Lorries had replaced the barges, and buses had replaced the 'Kitley Belle'. Yachts, motor launches, and sailing dinghies had replaced the old fishing fleet-boats were now becoming men's toys as opposed to being men's work-horses from which they made a living.

Although the 14ft regatta boats, built by Bill Tope, were proving to be a success in making most of the rowing races more even, the regatta Committee realised that the Yealm Crabbers were falling into disrepair and needed to be replaced. They decided to look for more evenly-matched boats that would secure the future of the Greyback race. After much discussion, it was agreed that the Royal Navy at Devonport, Plymouth, was to be approached to see if four Montagu Whalers could be borrowed each year - which they kindly agreed to.

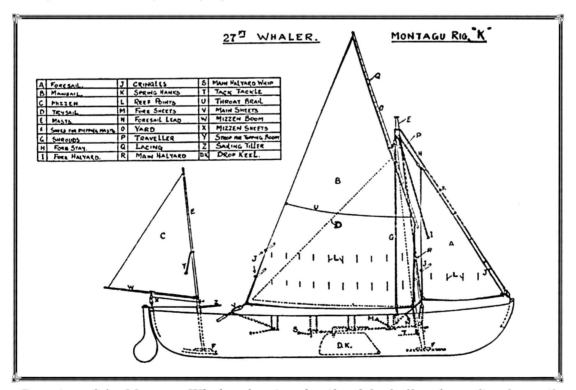

Drawing of the Montagu Whaler showing details of the hull and standing lug-sail rig (Admiralty Handbook, 1938).

The Whaler and the regatta

During the late 18th century and throughout the 19th century the Royal Navy adopted the Whaleboat, or 'Whaler', as the smallest ships boat that could be hoisted onboard by hand rather than by crane. At the turn of the 19th century, Admiral Victor Alexander Montagu CB (1841-1915) modernised the basic open-boat design of the Whaler to increase the beam, include a centreboard, and add a more suitable standing lug-sail rig with mizzen mast. This modified design was known as the 'Montagu Whaler'. It was 27ft long and intended to be sailed, or rowed with five oarsmen and a cox. Although heavy, it rowed well due to its good length and sleek hull. It was built by many Navies and Admiralty contractors around the world, becoming an internationally recognised and popular boat.

Everett Leonard (1912-1980) from Noss Mayo, was particularly instrumental in bringing the Whalers to the Yealm regatta. However, the switch from the old working Crabbers to the Whalers was not a straightforward process. Much arguing broke out in the lead up to the 1945 regatta. A number of people were keen to repair the remaining Yealm Crabbers or build some new ones. In reality, the idea of continuing with the Crabbers was impossible as money was very short after the war. Everett decided to settle the argument by burning the family Crabber, 'Emma-Jane', in Noss Creek. She was one of the last remaining Crabbers and was in a very poor state of repair. The way was then open for Whaler racing on the Yealm. I think the following memories, by Mike Leonard-Williams of Noss Mayo, highlight Everett's dedication to the regatta over many years, and provide an example of the considerable time and effort required by volunteers to maintain the regatta as a popular event.

1974 Everett Leonard manoeuvring two Whalers off the Yealm Yacht Club.

Memories of the Regatta

"Not being a "local" my memories of the Regatta only go back thirty years. At that time the Greyback race was rowed in 5-oared Admiralty Whalers, which being painted grey were mistakenly referred to as the "Greybacks". (The original "Greybacks", I understand, were the crews of farm labourers who would compete against the fishermen in the years before the war). These Whalers were borrowed from the Navy at Jupiter Point, up the River Lyhner. Just before the heats, a team of volunteers would set off by sea, with sandwiches, flasks of coffee and other sundry refreshments led by Everett Leonard. Once at Jupiter Point, which was a Whalers' paradise, Everett would scuttle around the craft like an antiques expert at a house clearance sale, eyeing each one with deep suspicion. Each Whaler was slightly different and one never really knew whether Everett was trying to spot boats which were nearly the same, or picking out one or two rough ones in the hope that Noss would be lucky in the draw! Scores of oars would be lifted up, inspected, tapped with the knuckles, bent over the knee and either rejected or accepted. I doubt if the Naval Commanding Officer himself ever carried out such a searching inspection of his fleet.

Eventually the chosen fleet of four would be taken in tow to the Yealm with a volunteer on each tiller. Their rudders were surprisingly light and it is said that a skilled stroke oar could easily use his blade to flip the rudder of an adjacent competitor straight of the pintles. I doubt whether this ever happened though! On Noss beach at low tide the Whalers would undergo an even more thorough going-over with screwdrivers, mallets, scrapers and other probes being inserted into every nook and cranny. With each boat being slightly different the races were exciting as ever, with the added bonus that crews could blame the boat if they lost! It seemed to me that for years Noss must have had an unlucky draw.

I remember once that a couple of strapping young village maids boldly volunteered to field a "Ladies" crew. This immediately precipitated an extraordinary meeting of the Regatta Committee which roundly rejected the proposal with solemn pronouncements such as "if women tried rowing a Whaler they would probably die!" and perceptive "They'ms built all different to us blokes! There's bits that'd git in th'way! That's why they can't row Whalers." It was to be a few years before one of the Yealm's few remaining male bastions was broken and the ladies successfully competed in the four-oared Crabbers, which, incidentally, in my limited experience are far harder to row than the 5-oared Whalers. As a local Innkeeper is reputed to have said "Us's got better women rowers on the Yealm than the worst men rowers!"

Times have changed but the fun of the Regatta lives on thanks to the hard work of the volunteers who keep it going. We should be very grateful to them for giving us such an enjoyable time every summer."

(Yealm Regatta Programme, 1999)

37

1963 Men's Greyback race. The boat in the lead, here rounding the International Paints' buoy, went on to win the race. The crew are Cox. J. Tope, Str. H. Hockaday, J. Roe, J. Hockaday, M. Farleigh, and G. Bennett.

Expanding programme of events

Throughout the late 1940s, 50s and 60s the regatta programme of events was gradually expanding. Competition was as keen as ever, and now fairer than before - with pairs and singles rowing in the Tope-built regatta boats, and the Greyback Race in the Whalers, loaned from the Royal Navy. As well as a full programme of rowing, swimming and sailing events, other more unusual events were taking place, including the shovel tug-o-war (in 14ft regatta boats), the water-borne pillow fight, the outboard motor race, and the best decorated boat competition. The outboard motor race was particularly challenging. It required considerable speed and boat-handling skills as competitors had to stop and start their Seagull outboards to retrieve a number of objects floating at different points around the course. The winner was the person who retrieved the most objects in the quickest time.

On-shore events were always an important part of the regatta. During this period, these included the open-air dance in Noss square, which was regularly headlined by Frank Fuge and his dance orchestra, the fair, which used to set up on the beach at the end of Noss Creek, and the children's fancy-dress parade, which demonstrated both childrens' and parents' creative talents.

Pete Stitson as a Swan!

One particularly enjoyable aspect of the regatta was the visiting silver bands, which used to play on a Saturday afternoon as the rowing events proceeded. On one occasion, Den Shepherd recalled that the Yealmpton Silver Band was persuaded to play aboard the old International Paints' barge, moored in the creek. After a while people realised that the music had stopped, and the barge was sinking fast. A hectic rescue operation ensued to get all the band members and their instruments safely ashore. In following years, the regatta Committee decided that the bands should play from the Pallot's garden at Riverside Road West, Newton Ferrers, thus ensuring that their Trumpets and Tubas stayed dry!

1976 view of the Plymouth Silver band playing in the Pallot's Garden, Newton Ferrers.

39

The regatta sailing events became more popular during this period as people started to acquire their own sailing dinghies. In the 1950s, three classes of dinghy were prominent in the Yealm - the Mayflower, built by Skentelberys of Plymouth, the International 14 and the Redwing. The latter two were designed by the famous Uffa Fox, and were popular in many parts of the West Country.

C.1950 regatta sailing race, featuring the International 14s 'Santoy' (K582) Robert Baker and Jack Shepherd, and 'Quickstep' (K355) John Hockaday and crew, the Redwings (139 – second from right) J. Threlfall and crew, and Jack Nicholson and crew (far right). Note that the fisherman stand-up rowing, in the background between the sails, is Harold Sims.

The photograph (courtesy of the Western Morning News) on the opposite page accompanied the following Western Morning News article from the 1954 Yealm regatta.

"The 1954 Yealm regatta will be long remembered as an outstanding success, for most of the events were carried out during a few brief and exceptional spells of fine weather. The sailing events were held on Monday the 9th of August the wind was very light and sailing was exceptionally good considering the conditions. Most exciting of all the racing was the 14ft 'International Race', in which all the first three competitors were within a few yards of each other on the second lap."

40

1954 Regatta sailing race, featuring (K625) Bob Andrews and Jack Shepherd, (7) Mike Parsons and crew in a Cooper 14 class, (K582) Robert Baker and Harry Hockaday sailing out of Noss Creek - late for the start as usual!

John Hockaday in 'Quickstep' was unlucky on the mark and was left behind. On the final lap he nearly caught the second boat. A truly thrilling race. Young Peter Court-Hampton made quite a good time in 'Petrel' in the cadet class. The outright winner of all events was Michael Parsons in 'Santanita', who just left most of the other craft standing. The prizes were to be presented on Wednesday by Mrs Lucy Tope.

Regatta Sailing Results
14ft International - 1 R. Baker (Santoy II), 2 S. R. Andrews (Timeetah), 3 J. Hockaday (Quickstep).
12-14ft Handicap - 1 M. Parsons (Santanita), 2 D. Court-Hampton (Watermusic), 3 M. Logan (My Minx).
Cadets Class - 1 P. Court-Hampton (Petrel), 2 P. Taylor (Lillibet).
Mayflower Class - 1 Gaskell-Brown (M18), 2 J. Nicholls (Sitch), 3 A. Spence (Woodcut)."

(Western Morning News, August 1954)

As the 1950s progressed, the Berker family of Casa Del Rio, Newton Ferrers (and Berkertex clothing fame), became very involved in the Yealm regatta. They presented some fine trophies that are still being competed for today. Some of these include: The Lesley Berker Trophy, for the most successful competitor; the Joan Berker Trophy, for the most sporting competitor; the Boys Perpetual Challenge Cup under 16; Boys and Girls Cup under 16; and Girls Perpetual Challenge Cup under 16.

Dave Walker of Newton Ferrers recalled that, as a young lad, on regatta rowing finals day he was gainfully employed by the Berker family to helm a launch hired from Frank Austin (who lived in the old Lifeboat house). He would turn up at Casa Del Rio's quay about an hour before the finals, and Mr and Mrs Berker would step aboard, immaculately dressed. Dave would then cruise round the course, ensuring that Mr and Mrs Berker always had a prime view of the day's events, before returning them home to Casa Del Rio in the late afternoon, whereupon Mr Berker would pay him the princely sum of 2/6d (12.5 pence in new money). After all the regatta events had finished, the Berkers would throw a grand party for all the competitors and people connected to the regatta. I believe it was always well subscribed as the food and drink was nothing but the best. One of the specialities was the sea food paella, which was prepared by Lesley Berker's own chef specially flown in from Spain.

C.1963 Yealm regatta prize giving. The trophies shown on the table include some of those presented by Berker family. Presenting the prizes is Mrs Pallot, then left to right Claire King (nee Gateley), Jack Tope, Harry Hockaday, Barbara Hemming, and John Leonard.

As usual, the decisions of the race starters and officials during this era could be controversial. This is highlighted in the following tale from the 1958 Regatta, recounted by Maurice Farleigh.

Tale of a Bygone Regatta

"In the 1958 Regatta the committee in their wisdom and as a matter of courtesy invited the Commanding Officer of R.A.F. Collaton Cross to be the starter and in command of the gun, ably assisted by Dickie Tope.

The youth's Greyback race started and finished without a problem and this race was closely followed by the men's Greyback race.

The race was started and all well. Returning back from the Paint Company buoy cox Jack Tope's Newton crew were leading as they approached the committee boat on their way to Bridgend and back.

Jack's boat was failing fast and being overhauled by Gerry Sims Noss boat and when the Newton boat passed the committee boat the good Commander fired the gun. This was a welcome relief to the near exhaused Newton crew (of which I was one) and they shipped oars and claimed a victory. Cox Gerry Sims in his Noss boat went past shouting abuse at the Commander and Jack Tope and completed the course.

The arguing about the race went on well into the late evening in the local pubs with tempers being raised. The final outcome was a re-run on the Monday evening when justice was done and the eventual winner was Gerry Sims and his Noss crew."

M.C. Farleigh

(Yealm Regatta Programme, 1994)

Soon after this incident, the difficult task of race starter was taken on by Gordon Princep Versailles 'Johny' Stitson (1919-1995), who continued as official regatta race starter from 1960 to 1980. Johny, as he was best known, was born at the end of WWI, when the Treaty of Versailles was signed, hence his name. He first came to Noss Mayo in the 1920s for summer holidays with his family, staying first at Stoke Camp (at Stoke beach), then at the cottages opposite the tennis courts in Noss Mayo. In the following years, he became great friends with Jack Shepherd, and when WWII broke out, the pair of them enlisted together.

Johny eventually joined the Parachute Regiment, and took part in the famous battle of Arnhem, where very heavy losses were inflicted on the allied forces. Eventually, the allies moved on to victory in Berlin, from where Johny was transferred to Palestine, just before the end of the war. When he returned to Noss Mayo, he married local girl Vera Pearce, and together they built their own house in which they lived for nearly 50 years and which continues to be Vera's home today. When Johny became the official Mr Starter, the regatta was a one week affair of rowing, swimming and sailing. He also officiated at events such as running, water-borne pillow fighting, tug-o-war, and on one occasion a ladies vs men's football match.

C.1961 Water-Borne Pillow Fight situated off the Pallot's Garden.
Johny Stitson looking on in his capacity of official starter and referee.

During regatta time Johny was a familiar face walking down Noss church steps carrying the famous 12-bore shotgun, whistles, and a bag with his thermos flask and sandwiches. Asked for her memories of these times, Vera Stitson said Johny must have been the only starter who was always late, probably because he had mislaid his whistles. Johny was also well known for shouting to rowers edging up on the start line 'It's no good any of you trying to get a flyer – all back!'. Johny was a firm supporter of the regatta for many years and kept a very sharp eye on all the events and competitors.

1976 Johny Stitson after lining up the boats on the
start line with the loud hailer, fires the gun. Note
Nora Rolfe covering her ear!

Regatta in decline

As the regatta moved on into the 1960s, problems started to arise. The Committee was struggling to raise enough funding, interest was waning, and it was only due to a few stalwart Committee members and their extremely hard work that they raised enough money to keep the regatta going. Although there were undoubtedly others involved, I believe it was mainly John Hockaday, Everett Leonard, Barbara Waddell, Phyllis Meehan, Joan Taylor, and Johny Stitson who kept things afloat, by the skin of their teeth. Without them, the regatta would probably have disappeared for good.

Although the regatta was in decline, there was still a core of keen competitors that continued to race, and the programme of events was largely maintained. The Tope-built wooden regatta boats were, however, showing signs of ageing, and proving more difficult to maintain as each year passed. This was mainly due to weakened fastenings and split planks, which caused the hulls to leak freely.

45

1963 Men's Challenge Cup winner, Harry Hockaday.

1969 Stand-up Rowing race - 1st Harry Hockaday, 2nd Rodney Carter,
3rd Mark Wilson.

To illustrate the difficulties faced by the regatta Committee during this time, it is worthwhile to include here some extracts from the minutes of the 1964 meetings, which were held to decide whether the River Yealm regatta had a future.

"Thursday 1st May 1964

Regatta AGM was held at the Tilly Institute at Noss Mayo the meeting was poorly attended so on the proposal of group Captain T. G. Horner and seconded by Mr E. Leonard another meeting should be called for on Thursday the 21st May at the new village hall, Noss Mayo. Posters to be printed and well advertised around the villages. The press to be notified of the forthcoming meeting. At that meeting it will be decided whether there will be a regatta in 1964!

An extrodinary meeting was held at the village hall on 21st of May 1964 8.00pm about 40 people present. Mr J. Hockaday was in the chair he fully explained why this meeting had been called for, and after a very full discussion took place about running a regatta the people present were all in favour that the regatta should be held this year. At this point a new committee was duly elected and the next meeting was called for on the 28th of May at the Tilly Institute".

1965 Prize winners with their cups. Back row from left to right P. Taylor, P. Meehan, ?, N. Kerley, B. Waddell, R. Stanbury, J. Travis, R. Carter, P. Gateley, C. King, K. Meehan, M. Wilson, T. Taylor, R. Jillard, ?, C. Carter, H. Hockaday. Children in the front left to right S. Meek, P. Hemelick, P. Stitson, N. Bourton, S. Tubb, N. Young, T. Meek.

Hopefully, in future years the regatta will not get to such a low point again. If people keep coming forward to join the Committee and help in other ways it will carry on to create a lot of fun for competitors and spectators, young and old.

New boats, new enthusiasm

It seems there was a gradual turning point in the late 1960s, when the regatta started to become popular again. I believe this was mainly due to the enthusiastic group of young people growing up in the locality at the time, who became involved in all aspects of the regatta. By the early 1970s, there was talk of building five new 14ft regatta boats to replace the old wooden ones. I remember there being considerable debate going on about the type of boat that should replace the old ones. Eventually, it was generally agreed that a boat belonging to Everett Leonard, and built by his brother Lando in the 1920s, should be the model for the replacement. This boat now belongs to Peter Leonard, Everett's son, who has recently told me that "a lick of paint, a few small repairs, and she could soon be on the water" not bad for a boat nearly ninety years of age.

After the calling of an Extraordinary Meeting in 1972, it was agreed that Hockaday Brothers of Membland would build a mould from the Leonard's boat, and construct five new boats in Glass Reinforced Plastic (GRP). These were eventually launched for the 1974 regatta, and are still in use today. These new boats certainly created a renewed enthusiasm and more young people were getting involved. The number of entries was steadily increasing throughout the 1970s, and heats for the races were quite a lengthy affair. Initially, they were held at Bennett's Quay, in the Kitley branch of the Yealm, before moving to Newton Creek, first at Kiln Quay (c.1983), and finally on up to Newton Brook (c.1989), where the tidal flow had less influence on the racing.

As well as the renewed enthusiasm for the Yealm regatta, local people were also keen to compete in other regattas in the region, particularly Dartmouth and later Salcombe. I believe the first time that rowers from the Yealm started competing in these regattas was at the Royal Dartmouth regatta in 1971 (see box on Excursion to Dartmouth regatta).

The forming of the Newton and Noss Amateur Theatrical Society (NNATS) in 1972 also livened-up events, with theatrical players such as Mike Leonard-Williams, Alan Baldwin, Tony Tubb, and Barry Furzeland, causing mayhem on and off the water. I believe at that time certain members of the regatta establishment did not always appreciate the NNATS sense of humour, as quite often is the case with the generation gap. As the 1970s unfolded the NNATS' certainly left their stamp, with their lively summer shows which raised lots of money for the regatta, and their varying success on the water.

Excursion to Dartmouth Regatta

In 1971, two Whaler crews travelled to Dartmouth regatta to represent the River Yealm in the Open Whaler race. One crew was from Newton, coxed by Brian Hockaday, and the other was from Noss, coxed by Den Shepherd. I remember taking a keen interest in this race, because a few weeks before I was lucky enough to be asked to cox the Newton crew during a practice session in a Whaler borrowed from Devonport dockyard. I was just 12 years old at the time and thoroughly enjoyed getting a free tour of the dockyard, which in those days was heaving with a multitude of ships from NATO forces.

The last Friday in August was race day, and I remember arriving in Dartmouth and walking off to the higher ferry to watch the start of the race. In contrast to the Yealm regatta, Dartmouth is a Royal regatta, and quite a large affair. Competition was very strong, with about 20 crews having entered the Open Whaler race, and only 6 finalists, including the two Yealm crews, lined up at the start. As the gun cracked off and the Whalers charged down the Dart, a very professional running commentary was describing the progress. The commentator, who was obviously pro Dartmouth, announced that a couple of Dartmouth crews had taken up a good lead, progressing down river towards the finish. At the half-way mark, I was running down the quay side following the race, and noticed the commentator was losing his enthusiasm, as the Newton and Noss crews were starting to challenge the leaders. By the time I had reached the finish line, off the Dartmouth Yacht Club, the commentator was faltering as he solemnly announced that Newton had come in first and Noss second. A great victory for the Yealm crews on their first ever outing to Dartmouth, and a real credit to the high standard of rowers from the Yealm. The winning crew was Newton Ferrers - Cox Brian Hockaday, Str Mark Wilson, Rodney Carter, Harry Hockaday, 'Gubby' Williams and Chris Carter.

1971 winning Newton Greyback crew, Cox R. Wilson. Rowers pictured in this crew also won at Dartmouth regatta.

*1976 NNATS on the water, part 1! Enter stage left to right Tony Tubb,
Tony Maskell, Mike Leonard-Williams, Alan Baldwin and Barry Furzeland.*

*1976 NNATS on the water, part 2! Enter stage left to right Barry Furzeland, Tony
Maskell, Tony Tubb, Alan Baldwin and Mike Leonard-Williams.*

1976 Dame Sybil Ives Academy for Young Gentlemen arriving to take part in the Men v Women Football Match.

1976 Regatta Football Team line up. Left to right B. Furzeland, P. Gateley, K. Meehan, M. Cawse, R. Williamson, P. Southcombe, M. L-Williams, P. Stitson, N. Taylor, P. Carter and A. Baldwin.

The Greyback race continued through the 1970s, being keenly contested by crews under the watchful eyes of wily coxes such as Harry Hockaday, Len Carter, Gerry Sims, Dennis Steer, John Hockaday, Rob Wilson, Mike Leonard-Williams, and many others. Although each year produces race favourites, surprises have always occurred. One such occasion is triumphantly recalled by Tommy Taylor in the following account.

"The year Newton 'B' crew won the Greybacks

Towards the end of the "Whaler" chapter in 1972, a young, light and enthusiastic crew coxed by ferryman Derek Hockaday could be seen seriously practising in the creek. Johnny Lewis (Stroke), Tommy Taylor, Joe Lovelady, Peter (Trog) Williams, and Paddy Gateley were that crew with an average age of 22. They were all involved in outdoor work at the time and so had a good level of fitness. An appropriate and promising 'B' crew so it seems.

From the start of the race they were surprised how close they were able to hold on to the two "A" crews. Then came the opportunity that must be exploited. The leaders clashed oars rounding the buoy at International Paints. Newton 'B' took the turn wide and passed them both. They were in the lead! All they had to do was not to throw it away. They didn't, and were clear at the Bridgend mark and although pressed hard by the other boats, they were first over the line and got the gun. The result: 1st Newton, 2nd Noss, 3rd Newton, 4th Noss.

Early that evening, Monica Gateley who was delighted to have a son and a nephew in the winning crew hosted the team in the Reading room, where Arthur Lee had sent Champagne to begin the celebrations. At the prize giving Phyllis Meehan announced the results with two extra words, 'The winners of the 1972 men's Greyback race: Newton Ferrers 'B crew'. The success was all the sweeter for being the "B" crew!"

(Letter from Tommy Taylor, 2010)

1972 Newton Ferrers B crew Cox. D. Hockaday, Str. T. Williams J. Lovelady P. Gateley T. Taylor J. Lewis.

1972 Noss Mayo crew Cox. D. Shepherd, Str. C. Stafford, B. Taylor, S. Rowse, D. Steer, J. Leonard.

*C.1976 Noss (coxed by Harry Hockaday) and Newton (coxed by Len Carter) crews
jostling for position at the International Paint Buoy.*

*1975 Len Carter and his Newton crew in full flow Str R. Carter, M. Wilson,
T. Taylor, Gubby Williams, P. Carter.*

1971 start of the Greyback race. The Noss crew in the foreground are Cox. G. Sims, Str. G. Staddon, B. Parsons, W. Prynn, P. Stitson, ?.

1975 Greyback race, victory for Len Carter and his Newton crew.

The Famous NNATS Controversy - 1977 regatta Greyback Race
as told by Mike Leonard-Williams

In the mid 1970s it was sometimes a struggle to get Greyback crews. We were then racing borrowed Whalers from HMS Raleigh which required 5 oarsmen. Also practising was limited to only a few days before the heats. Mike Leonard-Williams was teaching at the school of navigation in Plymouth and arranged for some crews to practise in their Whalers. This was controversial, as other teams claimed they had an unfair advantage.

In 1977 the NNATS decided to enter the Greyback race as a Newton crew. This caused a bit of controversy, especially with the Newton A crew (coxed by Len Carter), because the NNATS cox Mike Leonard-Williams lived in Noss, not Newton (this was allowed in the rules at the time.)

Having reached the finals the NNATS and Newton A were drawn next to each other. Off Kiln Quay they were level and getting closer and closer. Suddenly the NNATS crew lost steerage way. Newton A stroke, Rodney Carter, had cunningly managed to dislodge the NNATS tiller with the blade of his oar. (A feat he still boasts about!). The situation was quickly recovered by Mike, but Len had now pulled ahead. The umpires saw the incident and disqualified Len.

The NNATS rounded the buoy at The Pool and actually managed to overtake Len on the way back up to Bridgend! Len subsequently appealed to the Committee and a special appeal tribunal was established that evening at the Tilly Institute under the skilled chairmanship of Michael Baldwin. Those involved gave evidence and the Committee deliberated long and hard, while a huge crowd waited outside for a decision. At last it came: Newton A were reinstated and the NNATS roundly condemned for their cox not

1977 Greyback race the winners (boat no 7)
H. Hockaday and crew.

living in Newton which was now against the rules as the Appeal Committee had also drafted a new rule which says that Greyback crews rowing for either village must be coxed by a person born in, or residing permanently in, the village he or she represents.

1977 The end of a busy regatta day, Len Carter in his ferry boat 'Marie' heading for home.

1976 Youths Greyback race, winning crew Cox. R. Penwill, Str. S. Cawse, T. Martin, M. Hockaday, N. Barber, P. Leonard

Newton v Noss Shovel Tug-o-war crews digging in.

Giles Courtis looking relaxed after winning the under 16s Challenge Cup race.

1976 Pete Leonard and Raymond Penwill posing for the camera.

Diana Thery caught on camera by her sister Christine.

Regatta stalwarts on the Committee boat.

A fun fancy dress at Noss village hall.

Len Carter looking thoughtful.

Wendy Stitson looking forward to the race!

Young Phil Carter in the Sculling race.

Gubby Williams sporting an Edwardian hairstyle!

Newton Shovel Tug-o-war crew left to right I. Hemelick, R. Carter, C. Carter, M. Wilson, Gubby Williams and P. Carter.

Noss Shovel Tug-o-war crew, left to right M. Cawse, J. Leonard, B. Parsons, H. Hockaday, K. Meehan, B. Hockaday.

Wendy Stitson and Susan Taylor recovering from the ladies Shovel race.

Left to right Brian Hockaday (holding boot), Rodney Carter, Mark Wilson.

Simon 'skinny' Cawse winner of the 1976 fancy dress competition.

'Go on Mr Baldwin heave'

*1976 Tug-o-war. This crew will not be moved with Warwick Hemming
as anchor man.*

1976 Newton and Noss Amateur Theatrical Society Greyback crew.

The end of the Whaler era came in sight when, in 1978, the R.N. announced that the Whalers would no longer be available after 1979, due to cost cutting and changes to the types of small craft used in the fleet. The regatta Committee called for another Extraordinary Meeting, to be held in Noss Village Hall, to discuss the matter and consider options for the future of the Greyback race. A glimmer of hope did arise when it was brought to the attention of the Committee that Jim Hill of Bridgend had acquired a boat from Oreston, Plymouth a few years back. The papers he had concerning the boat revealed that she originally came from the Yealm, when she was owned by George Hockaday of Ferry Cottage, Noss Mayo. The boat's name was 'Shamrock'. Could she possibly be one of the old Yealm Crabbers? It was decided to investigate further.

Jim Hill had stored his boat in Hockaday's yard, Membland, where she lay, forgotten for several years, almost hidden by an assortment of boatyard debris. Two experienced 'old salts', Edgar Foster and Bill Hockaday, were set to work on the boat to decide whether she was an original Yealm Crabber. They had both worked on these boats and rowed them in many pre-war regattas. Much rubbish was cleared, paint scrapers were put to work, measurements taken, the hull shape was scrutinised, the old thwart positions discovered, the mast step revealed, and many serious discussions took place. Finally, it was announced that this was definitely the old Crabber, 'Shamrock', which had been built c.1890 in the cellar of the Round House, Noss Mayo, by John Hockaday.

C.1972 Jim Hill standing on the bonnet of his Woseley car as it is picked up by a big sitch which flooded the road at Bridgend - was Jim trying to create an alternative regatta event?!

Jim Hill was a skilled blacksmith and metal fabricator. Whether you required tailor made fittings for an old gaff-rigged yacht, or a shiny modern stainless steel balcony rail, Jim would always find a way of getting over the most awkward jobs. He was also a very keen sailor and fortunately his interest in boats led him to stumble across the Crabber 'Shamrock'.

The discovery of 'Shamrock' created a lot of interest, to the point that Hockaday Brothers of Membland decided to haul her into one of the boat sheds, carry out much needed repair work and prepare the old hull to enable a GRP mould to be cast from it. This news was made available to the regatta Committee of the time, and after much discussion at Extraordinary Meetings it was eventually decided that this was too good an opportunity to miss, and 4 new Crabber hulls were ordered from Hockaday Bros.

Lewis Hockaday (born 1968) sailing 'Shamrock'. Lewis is a direct descendant of 'Shamrock's' builder John Hockaday (1812-1906).

The main concern now was fund raising, and much activity occurred during 1979 and 1980 to raise the funds required for the new boats. The Committee worked very hard during this time, and it is particularly worth thanking the following people for their efforts: Maurice Farleigh, Barbara Waddell, the Leonard, Hockaday and Carter families. There were many others. Maggie Shepherd also played a vital part in the fund raising, organising grand fairs at Noss Village Hall on numerous occasions. As a result of this considerable effort, and the widespread support of people in Newton and Noss, the new Crabbers were ready for the 1981 regatta.

1979 was the last Greyback race competed for in the Whalers. Before this race commenced, spectators were treated to the grand spectacle of some veterans rowing the restored Crabber 'Shamrock'. Here, I thought it would be interesting to include some photographs of the veterans rowing 'Shamrock', and the commentary by Maurice Farlcigh explaining the scene at the time.

1979 Veterans preparing to row the Crabber 'Shamrock' up river.
Cox. Gerry Sims, Str. Joe Roach, Edgar Foster, Bill Hockaday and Everett Leonard.

1979 veterans rowing back up river towards cheering spectators.
Photographs courtesy of South Hams Newspapers.

Maurice Farleigh Commentary

"If you look towards the Yacht Club you will see that today we have something rather special for you, especially those of you who love to wallow in the nostalgia of old boats and old times. As you know, the forerunner of today's Whaler race was the Greyback race pulled in the old Crabbing boats of the Yealm. Alas, these grand old boats last raced here in the regatta of 1939, and have long since gone. But by a stroke of good fortune we have today the only remaining Crabber the 'Shamrock' which as it were, has been brought back from the dead. This boat, which was owned by the late George Hockaday of Ferry Cottage, has been recovered a near wreck and lovingly restored by the Hockaday Brothers to its original form. The men you see rowing her today are all men who in some way were involved with these boats, either by working them or rowing them in past regattas. The Cox today is 70 year old Gerry Sims who rowed in his father's Crabber, the' Eagle', many years ago and who for many years coxed one of the Noss Mayo Whalers. We have Joe Roach aged 78 years as Stroke, who pulled in various Crabbers and who won the Yealm Challenge Cup Singles outright in 1919, 1920 and 1921. Next we have Edgar Foster aged 77 years, who pulled in his family boat the 'Thistle' as well as earning a living from it. Edgar was the last man to sail a Crabber out of the Yealm fishing for a living. Next we have Bill Hockaday aged 70 years, whose family owned this boat and who pulled in the 'Thistle' during the age when the racing was really cut throat. Bill is also another outright winner of the Yealm Challenge Cup Singles in 1935, 1936 and 1937. Finally, we have Everett Leonard aged 67, who you all know has done so much for the Yealm regatta over many years. Everett used to row in his father's boat, the 'Emma Jane', and worked as a boatman here on the river for most of his life. There has been a GRP mould taken from this boat, and it is hoped that if enough funds are available, four of these boats will be built to replace the Whalers. What a grand site it would be to have the Crabbers racing again on the Yealm".

(Maurice Farleigh, Yealm Regatta Programme, 1979)

After the veterans had rowed superbly around a shortened course, the last Yealm regatta Whaler race took place. It was a tough-fought race but Noss could only manage second place - victory went to Len Carter and his Newton crew (pictured on the following page). The end of one era and the beginning of another.

1979 winners of the last Yealm regatta Whaler race. Stern to Bow: Cox. Len Carter, Str. Rodney Carter, Mark Wilson, Phil Carter, Tony Maskell, Andrew Hudson.

1979 Youth's Whaler race winning crew in boat no 3 were: Cox. Dave Sherrell, Str. Peter Leonard, Giles Courtis, Ian Sherrell, Steven Hockaday, Andrew Jennings.

1981 - 2009
Yealm Crabbers Reborn

As fundraising progressed through 1979 and 1980, a GRP mould had been cast from the old Crabber, Shamrock, and 4 hulls were then made. For the 1980 regatta, the Royal Navy kindly loaned four 18ft long cadet training boats, which were not the best of boats to row, but at least they kept the Greyback race going. Noss won this year, but competition was already starting to build up in expectation of the 4 new Crabbers, which were due to be ready for the following 1981 regatta. Come the early summer of 1981, 1 Crabber had been completed. This was closely followed by the other 3, which were being fitted out voluntarily by John and Pete Leonard, Rodney and Phil Carter, Jack Hockaday and myself.

Four new Crabbers

August 1981 arrived, and the 4 new Crabbers were ready! To mark the occasion, it was decided to hold a naming ceremony in Noss Creek, straight after the official regatta opening and fancy-dress parade on 14th August. Barbara Waddell, the regatta President, who had been passionate about the revival of the Crabbers, kindly agreed to name the new boats. The names are as follows: 'Shamrock II', 'Snowdrop', 'Emma Jane', and 'Thistle'. After the ceremony, many of the large crowd that had gathered departed to the pub, where much discussion took place as to which crews would be likely winners of the 1981 Crabber races. Discussions were no longer focussed solely on the Men's Greyback races, because for the first time the ladies were to race the Crabbers in the Yealm regatta. A fine, new trophy had kindly been presented for the ladies Crabbing boat race by The International Paints Company.

Barbara Waddell - 1913 - 1994

Barbara was licensee of the Dolphin Inn for 26 years and became a generous supporter of the regatta. In 1967 Barbara was appointed regatta President and was instrumental in organizing the first Beer race in 1972. Her support was much valued in 1979 when she generously donated funds for the building of 4 new Crabbers and it seems fitting that she was chosen to name the new Crabbers in 1981.

With the launch of the new Crabbers, the 1981 Yealm regatta was creating a lot of interest. Much practising was taking place in anticipation of the hard-fought races ahead. As finals weekend arrived, the sun was shining and conditions on the water were ideal for fast racing. Crowds of spectators lined the river banks, and craft of varying sizes and shapes carrying more spectators, were jostling for position to view the events.

The programme soon got underway, with Newton competitors excelling in the Challenge Cups - Barbara Hemming winning the Ladies Challenge and Mark Wilson winning the Men's Challenge. I remember thinking at the time Newton competitors were looking very confident of winning the Ladies Crabbing boat and the Men's Greyback races. As quite often is the case, the Yealm regatta always has a surprise or two in store. Nossites had other ideas, with convincing wins in both the Ladies Crabbing boat race and the Greyback race...the trophies were heading over to the right side of the river!

1981 winners of the Greyback race on Pope's Quay showing off their trophy!

The new boats had been tried and tested and they went down very well with competitors and spectators. The 1981 Yealm regatta had proved to be a great success, and everyone was looking forward to another year of sunshine and keen competition between Newton and Noss!

Sponsored row to Cawsands

Fundraising continued through the 1980s to help pay for the boats and the many oars required for them. It was decided to organise a sponsored row in the Crabbers from the River Yealm to Cawsands in Cornwall, a distance of approximately 6 miles. This event ran for several years, and regularly attracted a large number of people, probably in the region of 200. We would set off from Noss Creek with the 4 Crabbers and as we rowed down river an armada of small craft would join in. By midday we were approaching Cawsands having worked up a healthy thirst. I bet the landlords and landladies were rubbing their hands with glee, as they saw the fleet anchor close to shore and their landing craft descend on the beaches.

1988 start of the Cawsand Row, a crew in Elizabethan fancy dress!

1988 Eddy Grant (left), John Leonard (right) preparing to go ashore at Cawsands.

1988 preparing for the Cawsand Row.

1988 H. Hockaday (left), L. Carter (right) enjoying a pint at Cawsands.

1988 end of the day at Cawsands preparing for the return to the Yealm.

72

After one particularly fine day at Cawsands in 1988, the crew I was rowing with were getting ready to head back to the Yealm when Tony Maskell, a highly skilled and competitive oarsman, came alongside and challenged us to a race back to Popes Quay. This of course was duly accepted, and the race was on. Tony was rowing in his 13ft 6in Cornish Cove regatta boat which had a very good turn of speed. He set out on a tactical race, hugging the coast to Wembury through the inside of the Mewstone. We were roughly on the same course but a bit further offshore. Tony's tactics were paying off and as we approached the mouth of the Yealm it was a neck and neck race. In an effort to fend off Tony's challenge and put in a strong finish we were then ordered to up the stroke rate by our cox Harry Hockaday. It wasn't to prove that easy though as we had to fight hard all the way up river to Pope's Quay before arriving about 40 seconds ahead of Tony, pretty close for a 6 mile plus race. On arrival, Tony climbed out of his boat and up the steps onto the Quay where he collapsed in a heap. Resuscitation took place in the form of a serious fanning down and a pint of good ale! I thought that Tony's achievement of making it such a close race was a credit to his athletic prowess, especially as he had a drop of lubrication before the start of the race.

Whaler oars from South Georgia

After several years of highly competitive Crabber rowing, frequent breakages meant that oars were in short supply, and these were very expensive to replace. Fortunately, a keen supporter of the regatta, Rear Admiral Robin Hogg of Noss Mayo, was in a position at this time to acquire a number of suitable oars from a Whaling station over 7,000 miles from the Yealm. The following passage, written by Robin, describes how these oars were discovered and transported, courtesy of the Royal Navy, to the Yealm.

> "I was lucky enough to be appointed as Flag Officer 1st flotilla in 1985. A job that gave me administrative command of 30 destroyers and frigates, and, should an international crisis arrive, tactical command of Naval forces on operations outside the NATO area. This mostly meant the operational command of whichever aircraft carrier battle group was assigned to a particular task. It also meant that I was constantly monitoring events around the world in those areas that would fall to me in war.
>
> In the aftermath of the Falklands war, the Royal Navy kept a small force of warships permanently on patrol in the South Atlantic. In early 1986 I was called over the fleet satellite link by the Captain of HMS Liverpool who, with HMS Hermione and RFA Resource, was at that time patrolling in the South Atlantic, off South Georgia. The captain of Liverpool had noticed a large quantity of whaler oars lying in racks at the old abandoned whaling stations on South Georgia. I immediately sent him a signal as follows:

"FROM FOF 1
TO HMS LIVERPOOL, HMS HERMIONE, AND RFA RESOURCE.

Reference: SATCOM discussions FOF1/Liverpool.

1. I learnt today that there may be large quantities of discarded and unwanted Whaler oars at Grytviken and Stromness in S. Georgia.
2. If circumstances permit I would be grateful for as many as 50 if at all possible to be recovered for return to UK.
3. My intention would be to present them to the Yealm Regatta Committee for use at the annual regatta where 4 Crabbers have hitherto relied on RN Whaler/Cutter oars now no longer available.
4. If this proves feasible I will organise collection on arrival UK on advice from you."

The rest, as they say, is history. The Whaler oars were duly collected by Harry Hockaday and delivered to Noss Mayo where they were used for many years, if not for the regatta itself, during the weeks of Crabber training in the run up to the final competition.

Now, 23 years later, the last of these "windfall" oars have been broken by the many oarsmen who have made use of them over the years. They did, however, provide a real link with those hardy men from many countries who at the turn of the 20th century must have used them for Whaling, often in atrocious conditions.

Robin Hogg."

(Letter from Rear Admiral Robin Hogg, 2010)

Colourful, competitive and controversial

As each year in the early 1980s went by entries were steadily increasing, and I believe the highest number of entries for many of the races were recorded during these years. Popular events included the Ladies and Men's Challenges, Ladies and Gents, Ladies and Men's Pairs, and the Junior races. For the Men's Greyback race, up to 5 crews for Noss and 4 crews for Newton - 45 competitors, entered. Challenge Cup entries were also high, up to 25 for the Men's and about 15 for the Ladies. Many heats were required so that the number of entries could be whittled down to make the final line-up.

After the success of the 1981 regatta and the renewed enthusiasm, the 1982 regatta approached and competitors of all ages were to be seen practising intensely for several weeks prior to the finals. As usual, the Crabber crews were taking matters very seriously, and had embarked on rigorous training campaigns in anticipation of some hard-fought races. Spirits were running high! Regatta day arrived and all events were proving to be very competitive. The Ladies' Crabber final proceeded smoothly, with Noss taking the trophy for a second successive year. However, the Men's Greyback final was to be rather controversial. The race started with the 4 Crabbers charging off down river neck and neck with oars clashing and coxs shouting for water. Rivalry was particularly intense between Harry Hockaday's Noss crew and Rob Wilson's Newton crew, who were berthed next to each other. Rob's crew had the 3rd berth from Noss, which gave them water on the mark at the International Paints buoy. The Newton crew rounded first, but seemed to flag a bit as they headed back up creek. Seeing an opportunity, Harry pressed the Newton crew and tried to overtake, which proved impossible though as the Newton crew took a slightly convoluted course up river. The jostling continued until these two leading crews almost ended up ashore in Newton Brook! This was all too much for the race judge, Den Shepherd, who was frantically waving his arms at the Committee Boat to call a halt to the race. This was done with several shots from the famous 12-bore shotgun. The boats glided to a halt, the race was declared void, and in true regatta fashion heated arguments broke out all around. Eventually, after an Extroadinary Meeting on the Committee Boat, a re-row was scheduled for the Monday evening, which took place without further incidents, and Noss came home the winners. 1982 went down as another controversial year in the history of the Yealm regatta!

*1982 Ladies Crabber winners (whose conduct on the course, met with
the approval of the race judge) Cox. J. Shepherd, Str. A. Payne,
W. Cawse, J. Martin, W. Stitson.*

75

*1986 Ladies Crabbers winners Cox. T. Endicott, Str. J. Stitson, S. Hemelick,
D. Hemming, B. Hemming.*

*1985 winners with oars raised to
signal victory.*

*C.1987 Cox. S. Baldwin, L. Hocking, L.
Stone, J. Leonard-Williams, Lizzie Pyne.*

C.1986 Danielle Stone eyeing up the Sculling race course.

1983 Ladies Crabber winners Cox. J. Shepherd, Str. A. Payne, W. Grant, J. Martin, W. Stitson.

C.1998 preparing for the Under 14's Boys and Girls pair-oared race.
David Matthews Cox on the right.

C.1996 Ladies pub race crews smiling for the camera.

C.1999 Youth's Under 20's pair-oared race.

C.1999 Ladies Shovel race water fight in progress!

In the early 1980s the colourful and controversial aspects of the regatta were certainly given a boost when Val and Norman Doddridge became the landlady and landlord of the Swan Inn in 1980, and then the Old Ship Inn in 1985. Although they were running a very busy pub and restaurant, they were both keen followers of the regatta and wholeheartedly supported every event. All the pubs were packed to the rafters over the regatta period, and I particularly remember some great parties and sing-songs in the Swan and Ship during this time. Some memorable performers at these evenings were John Hockaday on his Accordion, and Pete Leonard singing his famous Thrashing Machine song. Norman revelled in controversy and was particularly skilful at stirring up some of the more enthusiastic competitors to boiling point. By the time the rowing finals came around many of these competitors were like coiled springs, highly motivated by Norman's mischievous comments over the previous few weeks.

In 1996, Norman took to the water proudly coxing the Noss crew to victory in the Men's Greyback race. The following year, Newton was victorious in this race, with John Shepherd coxing. However, 1998 saw the pinnacle of Norman's regatta career. Being one of Norman's crew I remember the day very clearly. The other crew members were Lewis Hockaday, James Baldwin and James Watkinson. We were getting our boat ready for the race and about to pick up our cox, Norman, from Point (opposite Popes Quay). As usual Norman was busy relieving himself behind a bush before stepping aboard. I never thought of him as someone of a nervous disposition, but Val assured me that he was when it came to coxing a Crabber. Out to the start line we went, lining up against the other

C.1982 Val and Norman Doddridge

crews. John Shepherd's crew were looking buoyant and confident. The start gun cracked off and John's crew pulled into an early lead by Kiln Quay. As we arrived at the first buoy (off International Paints) John's crew were rounding in first place, and he shouted to Norman 'See you at the finish, Doddridge!'. This had quite an impact on our crew, suddenly the boat surged forward and with each stroke we were gaining on John's crew. Returning past Kiln Quay and heading up to the Committee boat, we overtook John's crew in full view of all the spectators, and Norman shouted over 'See you at the finish, Shepherd!'. As we crossed the finish line in first place, Norman was beside himself with excitement, and couldn't wait to shake hands with John. It was an even bigger party at the Ship that night, when Norman announced that he was 'The greatest cox the River Yealm had ever seen!'.

Val and Norman carried on running the Old Ship Inn until the millennium. For 20 years they had entertained people involved in the regattas, creating a very lively atmosphere each time. Many people shared these years with Val and Norman, and I suspect they will probably not see the likes of this hospitality again.

The Beer Race is an unusual spectacle and unique to the Yealm. It was initiated by the NNATS, with the support of Barbara Waddell, in 1972, and in more recent years has been organised by Chris George, raising hundreds of pounds each year for St Luke's Hospice in Plymouth. The race comprises ladies and men's teams (6 members in each) which represent the various pubs and other establishments around the villages. The aim is for each individual team member to row between the three village pubs - the Dolphin, Ship, and Swan, and at each pub the ladies must drink a half pint, and the men a pint of beer. The winner is the team that completes the circuit in the quickest time. As you can imagine there are a number of casualties throughout the course of the race! But most seem to recover rapidly to carry on drinking throughout the evening, and are keen to return for more punishment the following year!

I remember the aftermath of certain beer race nights when most of the competitors would end up in the Swan. The drinking would carry on until Norman would shout 'drink up you b'zzzards and **** off!!'. Unbeknown to Val and Norman the evening was not over. A few survivors, mentioning no names, would start rounding up dinghies on the beach and, when all seemed quiet at the Swan, these would be carried up to the pub car park where they were deposited, along with any other nautical equipment to hand. This created a severe parking problem at the Swan the following day. Val and Norman always seemed to see the funny side of these antics, although I am sure Norman found a few choice words when he pulled back the curtains in the morning.

C. 1987 Beer race, Jane Stitson downing her beer at the Old Ship Inn.

C.2008 Beer race, Frederick Stitson facing red devil Simon Pratten .

81

Swan make it three in a row

● THE victorious Swan Ladies celebrate with licensee's wife, Mrs. Val Doddridge.

● A watery end for one oarsman.

● Third-placed Dolphin Men A — Warwick Hemming, Dominic Hussell, Dolphin licensee, Mrs. Babs Waddell, Guy Sommers and Rex Hillier.

THE Swan Inn, Noss Mayo, have developed a strange hold over the Yealm Beer Race — for they won the event this year for the third time in succession.

The pub's men's team won the race overall and the women's team drank their way to an impressive performance too, finishing well ahead of all their female rivals and ending up fourth overall.

And other competing team members jokingly resorted to revenge against the Swan landlord, Mr. Norman Doddridge, who was picked up by the defeated Newton and Noss Amateur Theatrical Society team, and thrown off the quay into the Yealm!

'The NNATS crew were so sure they were going to win,' he said, 'but as usual, we just rowed them off the river. It was the only way they could retaliate.'

'They have been telling me that they were going to run away with it for months,' he continued, 'but in actual fact they got thrashed!'

Mr. Doddridge was, of course, delighted with the performances of his teams and said that he would like to present another trophy and keep the one the pub already has.

The winning men's team comprised of Ian Simpson, Peter Leonard, Tony Martin, Peter Stitson, Giles Courtice and Michael Hockaday.

The victorious Swan ladies were Wendy Cawse, Wendy Stitson, Alison Payne, Jane Martin, Tanya Sherrell and Julie Shepherd.

President of the Yealm Regatta, Mrs. Barbara Waddell, said that the annual event went very well and was a 'good clean race.'

The final results were: 1 Swan Men; 2 NNATS; 3 Dolphin Men A; 4 Swan Ladies; 5 Dolphin Ladies; 6 Old Ship Men; 7 Old Ship Ladies; 8 Dolphin Men B; 9 Battisborough School.

Newspaper article courtesy of South Hams Newspapers 19th August 1983.

● A competitor downs a pint before embarking on another leg of the race.

● A scene from the race, outside of the Old Ship Inn, Noss Mayo.

PRIVATE NOSE

p i l . c k

ALL THE FINALISTS!

Aug. 3rd 1990 `VISA` Price 30p

REGATTA ODDS

Greyback Race:
Newton "A"	2-1 fav
Noss "B"	4-1
Noss "A"	10-1
Newton "B"	100-1 (4 ran)

Challenge Cup:
Cawse M.	10-3 (fav)
Wilson R.	4-1
Hockaday L.	50-1
Leonard P.	5-1
Martin T.	60-1 (5 ran)

No more stupid bets please. Ed

****

REGATTA SAILING
A great day on Saturday with no wind. Harry did it again by ramming the Committee boat at the start while Capt.Jennings (entrusted with the dreaded Red Crabber plus 15 stone outboard!) had a good lead to the first mark after which a tactical mistake led him to end up 5th overall having a good race up river against Susie's legs. Harry won (I think; he was too far ahead to see!)

****

TREASURE HUNT FIASCO!
Off we went in Jane Lethbridge's dad's dinghy armed with the impossible list of clues and very little intelligence between us. First to sea to get some strange flower, then we sped up the Kitley, passing Mrs.Phipps calmly sipping a G&T while Nicola feverishly tried for prawns in the weed. poor 'Petie' was at Steer Point reading the Notice in his 12 knot floating jacussi. Passing Shallowford Creek the engine whent 'phut' and Jane said "Oh! We've run out of petrol!" Amid girlish screams your editor rowed all the way back against the tide while Jill walked from the woods to Bridgend gathering clues and receiving severe facial injuries from Mr.Bewldwin's new car. Eventually on foot / under oars we arrived at the Quay properly knackered and humbly profered our dogeared form and sundry strange items. The items were checked and then we waited with bated breath to see if our answers were correct. To no avail. "What about the clues then?" I pleaded. "No point in checking *them* - you were 10 minutes late!" uttered a stern Mrs.Hussell. After *ALL THAT!* what a shock. So I nursed my sore arms and bum over a few pints while Jill nursed her sore legs and broken face, and Jane drank all the Armenac.
Oh, Alan Williams won, by the way.
Next year I'm going to get a huge crew together and station one person each at strategic points from Brixton to Stoke Point with a fast car near a phone, tell them what to get and then sit in the Swan and wait for the team to bring the clues in.

****

REGATTA SAILING
A great day on Saturday with no wind. Harry did it again by ramming the Committee boat at the start while Capt.Jennings (entrusted with the dreaded Red Crabber plus 15 stone outboard!) had a good lead to the first mark after which a tactical mistake led him to end up 5th overall having a good race up river against Susie's legs. Harry won (I think; he was too far ahead to see!)

YOUTHS GREYBACKS
While the unannounced Newton crew has been practicing in the dark under the watchful eye of Messrs.Phipps & Cox, rumours are abounding of the females in the Noss crew. This is not true. The nubile blonde cox is none other than Mark 'Leroy' L-W, well known clown of the Ship kitchens and eater.

POOR NICK IN PORNIC
Contary to last week's report, the Yealm Posers ran out of Gin not Tonic and put into Pornic where they drank themselves stupid for several days before Nick was sacked as cook and told to find his way home.
MEANWHILE: Capt.Lapthorn has taken his Gin Palace *Cef'n Brewer* down to the France to suppply Gin to the stranded Yachtsman at a cost of £55 a bottle.

Another 'Private Nose' edition by Mike Leonard-Williams packed with regatta stories.

83

C.1984 The Dolphin beer race crew. Left to right G. Galpin, W. Hemming,
D. Farleigh (kneeling), B. Gregor, D. Hussell, P. Squire.

C.1995 Beer race at The Swan. Chris Rhead (left) and Daisy Sherrell (right).

C.1986 Thomas Adlam at The Ship, its your round dad!

Danny Farleigh with alternative head gear!

The Best Picks

PRIVATE NOSE

p i l • C k

VISA Price 30p

CAWSE GIVING UP

As time after time victory slipped away from Martyn Cawse this Regatta the dejected bionic oarsman scowled into a near-empty pint pot and said "I think I will give up rowing now. I thought I was good and I might have been good. The problem is that I'm not, but its taken me 25 years to find out! However I am grateful to all my supporters who gave me so much encouragement over the years. It's a damned pity though that they've all moved away from the area." Mr.Cawse now intends to put all his effort into training his promising young daughter "Stalky" Cawse. As brother Simon said "The only chance the poor girl has is if she doesn't take a blind bit of notice of what he tells her. Anyway I can say anything now 'cos I'm going to live in Newton!"

LEWIS IS A HERO!

Lewis Hockaday, once written off as a rowing failure by Martyn Cawse, proved that he is now the best oarsman on the river by winning the Challenge Cup in style. Even Martyn admitted he was wrong "All I can say is he won. He came in first - I saw it. Therefore he won. Mind you he wasn't far off being second, and in my opinion if he hadn't won that's where he might have come in. " "That's more than Cawse ever did!" said a delighted Lewis. "I don't even think the prat's ever even qualified for the finals!"

SAILING CUP GOES TO NOSS!

Saturday's sailing races provided much entertainment and sailing pundits and yautties were dumbfounded by the winner of the much-coveted Bellingham Cup. This went to Graham Staddon sailing his Whaler . Poor Graham was on Pope's quay when the 10 minute gun went, still without a crew. He grabbed the nearest spectators and bore off to the starting line leaving several confused and shocked wives on the quay. As he crossed the line, onlooker John Watkinson, who knows about such things, observed that Graham's Jib was upside down. He conveyed this news to the crew who seem unperturbed by it. The boat proceeded round the course and won on handicap. Since then several keen sailors have been seen secretly trying sailing with their sails inverted. John Leonard nearly sailed round with his entire boat upside down!'Lack of Ballast!' said landlord of Yauchttie Pub "the Swan".

Snout

"I said we should never have allowed 'Private Nose' sponsorship into the regatta"

EXTRAVAGANZA PLANNED FOR REGATTA OPENING NIGHT
The regatta committee have promised a grand opening for the 1984 Nossangeles Regatta. To be performed by none other than Councillor and well known commentator Dennis Shepherd, the opening will involve 2 village hall pianos the entire regatta committee and a live ferret. Thousands are flocking into the villages for the event, the climax of which will be the first live performance in this country of shaking Southcombe and Rupture Club. 'Shaky' said "well man, i'm like ready for anything!". Members of the catering and hotel trade have been inundated with bookings, even the harbour masters office has been pressed into use as a four star double suite.

"I said 'Shove the oar in the _rollocks_'!"

Cartoon by Brenda Pratten

Graham's sailing manual has sold like hot cakes.

Sailing cup goes to Noss (Private Nose)

Throughout the course of the 1980s and 1990s, different events were added to the regatta programme, attracting more and more people each year. These included the Raft race, Fishing competition, Crabbing competition, Water-borne treasure hunt, Cricket matches, Tennis matches, Golf, and Mini Marathon. The Crabbing Competition, Treasure Hunt and Raft Race were probably the most popular events of the whole regatta.

Oscar and Ilana Hill enjoying the fishing competition.

1992 Treasure Hunt. Left to right M. Francombe, Jess Francombe, M. Hockaday, A. Hockaday, Joe Francombe.

1993 Treasure Hunt night. Stern G. Francombe, Mid-left to right S. Olsen, A. Hockaday, A. Cawse, N. Gibb, Bow S. Olsen, Jess & Joe Francombe.

The Water-borne Treasure Hunt was devised by Mari and David Hussell and became part of the regatta Programme in 1988. Year after year it draws a large armada of boats with their teams of clue solvers and young runners ready to hunt out vital information and treasure at varying points around the Yealm. Any visitors wandering around at this particular time must think the competitors are crazy, as they would observe boats of all shapes and sizes racing to different points of the river, with out-board engines revving, and eager crews jumping ashore to hunt out treasure. Finally, the treasure hunters congregate around Popes Quay, where question sheets and treasure are presented and scrutinised by the judges. Eventually, a decision is made and the winners are announced. There is one small drawback with being the winning team - you are awarded the prize of devising and setting the following years' treasure hunt, a challenging task for anyone!

The Crabbing Competition started in 1995 and is held at Popes Quay. It always seems to attract a large number of entries, ending up with standing room only. Young people line the edge of the Quay, dangling their crabbing lines into the water and hauling hungry crabs up into their buckets. It must be one of the oldest forms of seaside entertainment, and keeps everyone happy for hours.

Crabbing competition at Popes Quay.

The Raft Race is one of the more colourful events of the regatta. Many intricately designed rafts are assembled in various back yards and sheds around the villages, and brought to Newton Brook on race day. This motley armada is decorated with colourful flags and elaborate design features, and lined up for the start. The gun is sounded and eager crews frantically paddle their craft in the general direction of the finish line at Popes Quay. However, several of the rafts often have serious design flaws, and their crews eventually resort to swimming, with raft remains in tow, to the finish. The race not only provides youngsters with a lot of fun on the day, but also entertains whole families for days, if not weeks, beforehand.

1996 Raft race, featuring the groovy reggae raft.

1996 Raft race, featuring the Carribean crew.

1995 Pete Stitson overseeing the Raft race.

The fireworks display has always been an important and colourful event in the regatta. Over the years, it has taken different formats from the early days when Mr and Mrs Archie Nelder held the grand display at Warren Point on the Wembury shore of The Pool, to the present professionally-organized displays set off from a raft moored at Newton Brook. In intervening years, however, some regatta fireworks displays were organized by volunteers from the villages, and they certainly encountered some technical, but entertaining, problems.

Several memorable occasions spring to mind, when pyrotechnic experts such as 'Bear' Cassidy, Tony Martin and Dominic Hussell were in charge of these grand displays. One particular piece of explosive wizardry occured during a rocket launch, when instead of the anticipated vertical take off, it started behaving like an Exocet missile, hom-

Recent Yealm regatta fireworks display.

ing in on a target at Pillory Hill, Noss Mayo. It smashed straight through the window of an elderly lady's residence, terrifying the poor woman who had been quite happily watching the display until this moment !

Undoubtedly, the greatest finale to a regatta fireworks display was created by 'Bear' Cassidy. His pyrotechnic expertise excelled when he placed a 9in mortar into its launching tube upside down. He lit it, stood well back and dazzled the huge crowds with his pure genius! It exploded and rose to an altitude of approx. 25ft, whereupon it exploded again and showered the crowds along Riverside Road with gold stars. Everyone thought this was amazing and cheered enthusiastically. Bear (who has since been known by many as 'woosh-bang Bear') then downed another pint of lager, probably thought 'they had a lucky escape', and I am sure was already planning the next years' grand fireworks display.

Judging by the current popularity of all the regatta events, they look set to carry on for many more years. Having such a variety of events creates opportunities for most people to take part in some aspect of the regatta. This is a credit to the Committee and helpers who work so hard to keep all the events going. Not easy when the programme now stretches over a two-week period.

21st century and beyond

Reflecting on the River Yealm regattas of 100 years ago, they were grand Edwardian occasions, with graceful paddle steamers, such as the Alexandra and Princess Royal, bringing hundreds of elegantly-dressed spectators from Plymouth, eager to watch competitors from the local communities battling it out on the water. Although the paddle steamers and Edwardian grandness have disappeared, a common thread which connects the regattas of then and now is that the regatta continues to be the most popular annual event held between the villages of Newton and Noss, drawing people together on and off the water. Throughout the current regatta programme there is something for most people to participate in - whether you choose to compete in the rowing, sailing and swimming races, partake in the more leisurely activities such as the Water-borne Treasure Hunt, Fishing competition, Crabbing competition, or join in as a dedicated spectator.

2003 Sherrell family's North Star in the foreground.

The River Yealm regatta is one of the finest in the Westcountry. Its unique location, with the villages of Newton and Noss facing each other across the narrow creek, forms a natural amphitheatre, encouraging the competitive inter-village rivalry which has always kept events alive, and caused controversy from time to time. This creates a vibrant atmosphere not easy to find in other regattas. I believe we are very lucky to have this unique situation.

Moving further into the 21st century, the challenge will be to uphold this long-running tradition for future generations. Newton and Noss have become very expensive residential areas. Young people growing up in these villages generally take the view that a future here is improbable as housing is unaffordable and good employment opportunities are scarce. If this situation carries on, young people will keep drifting away from the area and Newton and Noss will end up with an ageing population and a high percentage of holiday homes. This has already happened in many communities throughout Devon and Cornwall, and it has resulted in the loss of many traditional events, and villages being inactive outside of the holiday season. Projects to create affordable housing in Newton and Noss have been talked about for years and different ideas have been put forward, but very little seems to have been achieved. Looking on the positive side, considerable effort is still being made to address these needs. Affordable housing projects have been a success in other expensive residential areas, for example Rock in North Cornwall, so surely the same can be achieved within Newton and Noss. It is vital that this work meets with some success to ensure that the villages remain interesting and lively places in which to live, and future generations of enthusiastic regatta organisers and competitors ensure that the River Yealm regatta is a success for another 100 years.

2004 Start of the Boys under 14's pair-oared race.

2004 Winning Ladies Crabber crew, Cox. Kelly Stock, Str. Amy Mann,
Claire Cassidy, Kairen Carter, Debbie Hemming.

2004 Winning Men's Greyback crew Cox. J. Leonard, Str. P. Leonard, J. Baldwin,
L. Hockaday, M. Hockaday.

2004 Junior Combination race Merryn Hockaday (green)
and Daniel Bowyer (blue).

2004 Youth's Crabber race, Cox. Kylie Carter, Str. Jack Carter,
Joseph Francombe, Natalie Gibb, Luke Rainbird.

2007 Cox. Jeremy Eason, Sam Dowling, Ted Carruthers.

2009 Greyback race, Cox. M. Hockaday, Str. J. Francombe, W. Stitson,
A. Danning, G. Grant.

2009 John Leonard 'Mr Starter'.
Ready for more action in 2010!

2007 Winning Greyback crew,
T. Martin, A. Danning, Str. P. Stitson,
W. Mumford, Cox. P. Francombe.

2009 Winning Newton Ladies Crabber crew.

2009 Winning Ladies Crabber crew, left to right Cox. S. Taylor, K. Carter,
S. Bradford, Str. H. Adlam, N. Gibb.

2009 Winning Newton Greyback crew, left to right C. Rhead, Str. C. Matthews, Cox. P. Carter, J. O'Brien, J. Shepherd.

2009 Men's Challenge cup winners going back to 1952. Left to right H. & L. Hockaday, P. Leonard, D. Shepherd, M. Wilson, R. Carter, M. Parsons, J. Baldwin, M. Hockaday, R. Cawse.

The following photo is of the 2010 regatta Committee.

2010 River Yealm regatta Committee members, left to right: Robert Parsons, Darrell Marshall, Peter Stitson, Jack Hockaday (Time Keeper), Alan Baldwin (Vice Chairman), Maurice Farleigh (Vice President), Tony Tubb (Chairman), Rodney Carter, Liz Stone, Paul Francombe, John Hockaday (President), Tony Martin, Wendy Uzzell, Debbie Rhead, Jan Leonard, Jane Martin, Jane Stitson (Hon. Secretary), Bob Jeffery. Missing is Jane Wain (Hon. Treasurer).

The Committee members spend considerable time and effort throughout the year to ensure that the River Yealm regatta is a success. Many have been involved with this task for several decades, and it is through all their hard work that we are able to enjoy the various events that make up the current regatta programme.

So, come on Newton and Noss, hang out your bunting, fill out your entry forms, get practising, and let's enjoy another River Yealm regatta. Good luck to all competitors...especially those from Noss!

APPENDIX

Many trophies have been presented for different regatta events over the years, which now makes the annual prize-giving a lengthy occassion. Alan Baldwin who presides over the event, swiftly calls the prize winners names out and the large table full of glittering trophies soon lightens its load. Once proceedings at either the WI hall or the Noss Village Hall are finished, the crowd eagerly move onto local hostelries, where prize winners fill their cups and regatta events are mulled over in great detail. On the following pages there are some rowing results which include the Mens Greyback race, the Ladies Crabbing Boat race, and the Mens and Ladies Challenge Cup races. I thought it was also worth mentioning the Bellingham Trophy for Sailing, detailed below is the story behind the trophy by Tommy Taylor.

"Arguably one of the most pleasing of regatta trophies is a memorial cup given by a family to remember a popular and well liked young man who if he were here today would be aged 88.

Lieutenant K. E. Bellingham, Royal Artillery, aged 22, Ken, died on the morning of June 6th 1944. He was shot while attempting to free a field gun that had become bogged down close to Sword Beach in Normandy. He is buried in the Commonwealth War Cemetery at Hermanville-sur-Mer. His name is honoured on both the Newton Ferrers Memorial and in the Yealm Yacht Club.

The Bellinghams had moved to Yealm Road, Newton Ferrers from Plymouth in the mid-1930s. Ken was an only child and also a precious nephew of two maiden aunts and a bachelor uncle who lived on Court Road. Ken's father Lt. Cdr J. E. (Jimmy) Bellingham was the Harbourmaster and thus Clerk of the Regatta Course.

Ironically, Ken had been badly injured in a car accident in Brixton in the spring of 1944 and had only been passed fit to return to his unit just a few days prior to D-Day.

Ken liked everything about the river. He sailed an International 14 and with this in mind the trophy was presented for the Fast handicap Class (then the premier event of the dinghy sailing scene). Until the 1970s there would have been competitors who sailed in the Bellingham Cup, who would themselves have sailed with Ken."

(Letter from Tommy Taylor, 2010)

Bellingham Memorial Cup

Ladies Challenge Cup

Men's Challenge Cup

Men's Greyback Cup

1911
' May Queen '
Cox J.T. Sims
Str S. Andrews
C. Rogers
J. Parsons
A. Easton

1912
' Thistle '
Cox W.M. Hockaday
Str J. Hodge
F. Foster
A. Nelder
V. Hodge

1913
' Thistle '
Cox W.M. Hockaday
Str C. Rogers
J. Parsons
A. Nelder
V. Hodge

1914
' Thistle '
Cox T. Algate
Str C. Rogers
J. Parsons
C. Tope
A. Nelder

1919
' Emily '
Cox R. Hockaday
Str J. Parsons
A. Tope
W. Tope
A. Roach

1920
' Emily '
Cox R. Hockaday
Str J. Parsons
A. Tope
W. Tope
A. Roach

1921
' Emily '
Cox R. Hockaday
Str S. Roach
A. Tope
W. Tope
A. Roach

1922
' Emily '
Cox E. Dyer
Str J. Parsons
L. Baker
R. Hodge
G. H Sims

1923
' Eagle '
Cox R. Hockaday
Str E. Hodge
V. Hodge *Jnr*
W. Tope
A. Roach

1924
' Lookout '
Cox G. Hockaday
Str S. Shepherd
P. Hockaday
S. Squires
G.S. Tope

1925
' Eagle '
Cox R. Hockaday
Str J. Parsons
V. Hodge *Jnr*
W. Tope
A. Roach

1926
' Lookout '
Cox W. Hockaday
Str S. Shepherd
S. Squires
P. Hockaday
J. Dyer

1927 (Newton)
' Emma Jane '
Cox H. Hockaday
Str P. Hockaday
J. Dyer
G. Hockaday
S. Squires

1928 (Newton)
' Emma Jane '
Cox H. Hockaday
Str P. Hockaday
J. Dyer
G. Hockaday
S. Squires

1929 (Newton)
' Emma Jane '
Cox H. Hockaday
Str P. Hockaday
J. Dyer
G. Hockaday
S. Squires

1930 (Newton)
' Emma Jane'
Cox H. Hockaday
Str P. Hockaday
J. Dyer
G. Hockaday
S. Squires

1931
' Eagle'
Cox S. Foster
Str G. Sims
R. Baker
R. Hodge
W. Tope

1932
' Emma Jane'
Cox E. Leonard
Str V. Hodge *Jnr*
L. Leonard
W. Finch *Jnr*
I. Parsons

1933
' Eagle'
Cox S. Foster
Str G. Sims
W. Tope
R. Baker
R. Hodge

1934 (Newton)
' Thistle'
Cox H. Hockaday
Str G. Hockaday
W. Hockaday
P. Hockaday
E. Foster

1935 (Newton)
' Snowdrop'
Cox G. Tope
Str W. Tope
J. Dyer
A. Roach
A. Tope

1936 (Newton)
' Snowdrop'
Cox J. Tope
Str W. Tope
A. Tope
F. Tope
G. Tope

1937 (Newton)
' Thistle'
Cox H. Hockaday
Str G. Hockaday
W. Hockaday
P. Hockaday
E. Foster

1938 (Newton)
' Snowdrop'
Cox J. Tope
Str W. Tope
A. Tope
F. Tope
G. Tope

1939 (Newton)
' Snowdrop'
Cox J. Tope
Str W. Tope
A. Tope
F. Tope
G. Tope

BREAK FOR THE
WAR YEARS 1945
ONWARDS
ROYAL NAVY
MONTAGU
WHALERS

1945 (Newton)
Cox A. Tope
Str L. Carter
J. Roach
E. Carter
D. Crowdon
C. Roach

1946 (Noss)
Cox S. Foster
Str R. Baker
J. Shepherd
N. Williams
E. Leonard
A. Aggett

1947 (Noss)
Cox S. Foster
Str R. Baker
J. Shepherd
N. Williams
J. Hodge
E. Leonard

1948 (Noss)
Cox E. Dyer
Str R. Baker
J. Shepherd
N. Williams
W. Tope
E. Leonard

1949 (Noss)
Cox G. Sims
Str R. Tatum
J. Gibbons
J. Stitson
D. Shepherd
P. Rowse

1950 (Noss)
Cox G. Sims
Str R. B. Tatum
J. Gibbons
J. Stitson
D. Shepherd
P. Rowse

1951 (Noss)
Cox J. Hockaday
Str R. Baker
J. Shepherd
N. Williams
W.J. Tope
E. Leonard

1952 (Noss)
Cox G. Sims
Str R.B. Tatum
J. Gibbons
J. Stitson
D. Shepherd
P. Rowse

1953 (Noss)
Cox R. Baker
Str J. Shepherd
E. Leonard
N. Williams
J. Hockaday
P. Leonard

1954 (Noss)
Cox G. Sims
Str J. Gibbons
J. Rowsell
D. Shepherd
J. Stitson
P. Rowse

1955 (Noss)
Cox J. Hockaday
Str R. Baker
E. Leonard
N. Williams
R. Cawse
J. Shepherd

1956 (Noss)
Cox J. Hockaday
Str R. Baker
E. Leonard
N. Williams
M. Parsons
R. Cawse

1957 (Noss)
Cox G. Sims
Str J. Gibbons
V. Payne
D. Shepherd
J. Stitson
P. Rowse

1958 (Noss)
Cox J. Hockaday
Str R. Baker
D. Pooley
B. Horn
R. Cawse
M. Parsons

1959 (Newton)
Cox J. Tope
Str H. Hockaday
J. Shepherd
W. Hockaday
J. Hockaday
M. Farleigh

1960 (Noss)
Cox G. Sims
Str M. Parsons
V. Payne
R. Cawse
D. Shepherd
J. Stitson

1961 (Noss)
Cox J. Hockaday
Str M. Parsons
R. Baker
R. Cawse
E. Leonard
P. Roe

1962 (Noss)
Cox G. Sims
Str T. Finch
R. Parsons
V. Payne
D. Shepherd
C. Bradley

1963 (Newton)
Cox J. Tope
Str H. Hockaday
M. Farleigh
J. Roe
H. Hockaday
G. Bennett

1964 (Newton)
Cox J. Tope
Str H. Hockaday
J. Hockaday
G. Bennett
G. Skentelbery
M. Wilson

1965 (Newton)
Cox M. Farleigh
Str H. Hockaday
J. Hockaday
P. Skentelbery
R. Carter
M. Wilson

1966 (Noss)
Cox G. Sims
Str P. Pearson
R. Parsons
T. Finch
W. Prynn
A. Harris

1967 (Noss)
Cox D. Shepherd
Str G. Staddon
B. Taylor
T. Pearce
D. Steer
J. Leonard

1968 (Noss)
Cox D. Shepherd
Str G. Staddon
I. Roberts
T. Pearse
B. Taylor
J. Leonard

1969 (Newton)
Cox R. Wilson
Str M. Wilson
R. Carter
H. Hockaday
B. Hockaday
B. Stock

1970 (Newton)
Cox R. Wilson
Str M. Wilson
R. Carter
H. Hockaday
B. Hockaday
C. Williams

1971 (Newton)
Cox R. Wilson
Str M. Wilson
R. Carter
H. Hockaday
C. Williams
C. Carter

1972 (Newton)
Cox D. Hockaday
Str T. Williams
J. Lovelady
P. Gateley
T. Taylor
J. Lewis

1973 (Newton)
Cox L. Carter
Str R. Carter
S. Williams
A. Martin
J. Endicott
C. Carter

1974 (Newton)
Cox L. Carter
Str R. Carter
M. Wilson
G. Williams
J. Endicott
C. Carter

1975 (Newton)
Cox L. Carter
Str R. Carter
M. Wilson
T. Taylor
N. Williams
P. Carter

1976 (Noss)
Cox D. Steer
Str B. Howson
D. Penwill
N. Taylor
S. Johns
P. Stitson

1977 (Noss)
Cox H. Hockaday
Str B. Hockaday
R. Parsons
M. Cawse
S. Cawse
J. Leonard

1978 (Newton)
Cox L. Carter
Str R. Carter
M. Wilson
T. Maskell
C. Carter
P. Carter

1979 (Newton)
Cox L. Carter
Str R. Carter
M. Wilson
T. Maskell
P. Carter
A. Hudson

1980 (Noss)
Cox H. Hockaday
Str P. Leonard
M. Cawse
M. Hockaday
J. Leonard

1981 (Noss)
' Shamrock'
Cox H. Hockaday
Str P. Leonard
M. Cawse
M. Hockaday
J. Leonard

1982 (Noss)
' Emma-Jane'
Cox H. Hockaday
Str P. Leonard
M. Cawse
M. Hockaday
J. Leonard

1983 (Noss)
' Snowdrop'
Cox H. Hockaday
Str P. Leonard
M. Cawse
M. Hockaday
J. Leonard

1984 (Noss)
' Snowdrop'
Cox H. Hockaday
Str P. Leonard
M. Cawse
M. Hockaday
J. Leonard

1985 (Noss)
' Shamrock'
Cox H. Hockaday
Str P. Leonard
M. Cawse
M. Hockaday
J. Leonard

1986 (Newton)
' Shamrock'
Cox C. Carter
Str R. Carter
A. Tubb
R. Parsons
P. Carter

1987 (Newton)
' Thistle'
Cox J. Shepherd
Str N. Shepherd
M. Wilson
M. Hemming
L. Hockaday

1988 (Noss)
' Shamrock'
Cox I. Sherrell
Str P. Shepherd
A Sherrell
S. Rogers
L. Finch

1989 (Noss)
' Shamrock'
Cox J. Hockaday
Str P. Leonard
M. Cawse
M. Hockaday
J. Leonard

1990 (Noss)
' Emma-Jane'
Cox J. Hockaday
Str P. Leonard
M. Cawse
M. Hockaday
J. Leonard

1991 (Newton)
' Thistle'
Cox B. Carter
Str R. Carter
M. Hemming
A. Tubb
J. O'Brien

1992 (Newton)
' Emma Jane'
Cox B. Carter
Str R. Carter
A. Tubb
M. Hemming
J. O'Brien

1993 (Newton)
' Snowdrop'
Cox B. Carter
Str R. Carter
A. Tubb
M. Hemming
J. O'Brien

1994 (Newton)
'Shamrock'
Cox J. Shepherd
Str N. Shepherd
M. Wilson
C. Rhead
S. Bowden

1995 (Newton)
'Thistle'
Cox J. Shepherd
Str N. Shepherd
M. Wilson
C. Rhead
P. Shepherd

1996 (Noss)
Cox N. Doddridge
Str M. Hockaday
L. Hockaday
K. Jones
L. Finch

1997 (Newton)
Cox J. Shepherd
Str N. Shepherd
C. Rhead
M. Wilson
P. Shepherd

1998 (Noss)
Cox N. Doddridge
Str M. Hockaday
L. Hockaday
J. Baldwin
J. Watkinson

2000 (Newton)
Cox J. Shepherd
Str N. Shepherd
C. Rhead
M. Wilson
P. Shepherd

2001 (Noss)
Cox J. Leonard
Str P. Leonard
L. Hockaday
M. Hockaday
J. Baldwin

2002 (Noss)
Cox J. Leonard
Str P. Leonard
L. Hockaday
M. Hockaday
J. Baldwin

2003 (Noss)
Cox J. Leonard
Str P. Leonard
L. Hockaday
M. Hockaday
J. Baldwin

2004 (Noss)
Cox J. Leonard
Str P. Leonard
L. Hockaday
M. Hockaday
J. Baldwin

2005 (Noss)
Cox P. Francombe
Str P. Stitson
T. Martin
K. Jones
W. Mumford

2006 (Newton)
Cox P. Carter
Str N. Shepherd
C. Rhead
M. Stock
J. O'Brien

2007 (Noss)
Cox P. Francombe
Str P. Stitson
T. Martin
W. Mumford
A. Danning

2008 (Newton)
Cox P. Carter
Str N. Shepherd
C. Rhead
J. O'Brien
C. Matthews

2009 (Newton)
Cox P. Carter
Str C. Matthews
J. Shepherd *Jnr*
C. Rhead
J. O'Brien

LADIES
CRABBER RACE
RESULTS

1981 (Noss)
' Emma Jane'
Cox K. Minto
Str L. Bayliss
T. Andrews
W. Cawse
A. Payne

1982 (Noss)
' Snowdrop'
Cox J. Shepherd
Str A. Payne
J. Martin
W. Stitson
W. Cawse

1983 (Noss)
' Shamrock'
Cox J. Shepherd
Str A. Payne
J. Martin
W. Stitson
W. Cawse

1984 (Newton)
' Thistle'
Cox T. Endicott
Str B. Hemming
S. Hemelik
D. Hemming
J. Stitson

1985 (Newton
' Shamrock'
Cox T. Endicott
Str B. Hemming
J. Stitson
D. Hemming
K.Gingell

1986 (Noss)
' Shamrock'
Cox G. Martin
Str A. Adlam
W. Cawse
J. Martin
W. Uzzell

1987 (Noss)
Cox J. Shepherd
Str A. Adlam
W. Cawse
J. Martin
W. Uzzell

1988 (Newton)
' Emma Jane'
Cox E. Hussell
Str C. Cassidy
S. Symington
K. Carter
J. Stitson

1989 (Newton)
' Shamrock'
Cox E. Hussell
Str C. Cassidy
F. Symington
S. Symington
J. Melvin

1990 (Noss)
' Emma Jane'
Cox K. Hockaday
Str T. Hoskin
D. Hockaday
G. Martin
J. Leonard

1991 (Newton)
Cox E. Hussell
Str F. Symington
C. Cassidy
K. Carter
J. Melvin

1992 (Newton)
' Emma Jane'
Cox E. Hussell
Str F. Symington
C. Cawse
K. Stock
J. Stitson

1993 (Newton)
' Snowdrop'
Cox E. Hussell
Str K. Stock
C. Morsman
K. Carter
J. Stitson

1994 (Noss)
Cox K. Hockaday
Str T. Hoskin
A. Adlam
J. Leonard
E. Bird

1995 (Newton)
' Emma Jane'
Cox B. Hemming
Str C. Cawse
F. Symington
D. Hemming
K. Carter

1996 (Noss)
Cox K. Hockaday
Str T. Hoskin
J. Leonard
A. Adlam
G. Martin

1997 (Newton)
Cox P. Shepherd
Str S. Symington
F. Symington
A. Mann
C. Cawse

1998 (Newton)
Cox G. Tubb
Str F. Symington
C. Cawse
D. Hemming
A. Mann

1999 (Newton)
Cox G. Tubb
Str F. Symington
S. Symington
C. Cawse
A. Mann

2000 (Newton)
Cox P. Matthews
Str F. Symington
K. Stock
C. Cawse
A. Mann

2001 (Newton)
Cox P. Shepherd
Str F. Symington
K. Stock
C. Cawse
A. Mann

2002 (Newton)
Cox K. Stock
Str A. Mann
J. Stitson
K. Carter
C. Cawse

2003 (Newton)
Cox K. Stock
Str A. Mann
C. Cawse
K. Carter
J. Stitson

2004 (Newton)
Cox K. Stock
Str A. Mann
C. Cawse
K. Carter
D. Hemming

2005 (Noss)
Cox L. Hocking
Str K. Peters
J. Longworth
E. Bird
J. Martin

2006 (Newton)
Cox A. Thompson
Str A. Mann
J. Stitson
C. Cassidy
G. Wilson

2007 (Newton)
Cox A. Thompson
Str A. Mann
J. Stitson
C. Cassidy
G. Wilson

2008 (Newton)
Cox C. Lytle
Str A. Mann
C. Cassidy
D. Hemming
D. Stone

2009 (Newton)
Cox S. Taylor
Str H. Adlam
N. Gibb
K. Carter
S. Bradford

Men's Challenge Cup Winners

1919	S.C. Roach	1946	E. Carter	1969	R. Carter	1992	M. Wilson
1920	S.C. Roach	1947	V. Hodge	1970	M. Wilson	1993	M. Wilson
1921	S.C. Roach	1948	L. Carter	1971	M. Wilson	1994	M. Wilson
1922	A. Nelder	1949	L. Carter	1972	M. Wilson	1995	M. Wilson
1923	V. Hodge *Jnr*	1950	F. Austin	1973	R. Carter	1996	L. Hockaday
1924	V. Hodge *Jnr*	1951	F. Austin	1974	R. Carter	1997	J. Baldwin
1925	V. Hodge *Jnr*	1952	M. Parsons	1975	R. Carter	1998	J. Baldwin
1926	V. Hodge *Jnr*	1953	F. Austin	1976	R. Carter	1999	M. Hockaday
1927	V. Hodge *Jnr*	1954	P. Leonard	1977	M. Wilson	2000	J. Baldwin
1928	S.C. Roach	1955	D. Shepherd	1978	R. Carter	2001	J. Baldwin
1929	L. Leonard	1956	R. Baker	1979	M. Wilson	2002	J. Baldwin
1930	L. Leonard	1957	M. Parsons	1980	M. Hockaday	2003	J. Baldwin
1931	L. Leonard	1958	H. Hockaday	1981	M. Wilson	2004	M. Hockaday
1932	E. Leonard	1959	H. Hockaday	1982	P. Leonard	2005	J. Baldwin
1932	E. Leonard	1960	M. Parsons	1983	G. Courtis	2006	J. Baldwin
1933	E. Leonard	1961	M. Parsons	1984	P. Leonard	2007	J. Baldwin
1934	E. Leonard	1962	R. Cawse	1985	P. Leonard	2008	J. Baldwin
1935	W. Hockaday	1963	H. Hockaday	1986	M. Hockaday	2009	J. Baldwin
1936	W. Hockaday	1964	R. Carter	1987	M. Wilson		
1937	W. Hockaday	1965	R. Carter	1988	P. Leonard		
1938	G. Tope	1966	H. Hockaday	1989	M. Wilson		
1939	W. Hockaday	1967	M. Wilson	1990	M. Wilson		
1945	L. Carter	1968	M. Wilson	1991	M. Wilson		

Ladies Challenge Cup Winners

1923	E. Hockaday (Tope)	1955	S. Bradley (Brook)	1982	B. Hemming
1924	E. Hockaday (Tope)	1956	S. Bradley (Brook)	1983	A. Payne
1925	B. Tope (Farleigh)	1957	M. Baker	1984	B. Hemming
1926	B. Tope (Farleigh)	1958	B. Stevens (Hemming)	1985	T. Andrews
1927	B. Tope	1958	B. Stevens (Hemming)	1986	J. Leonard
1928	B. Tope	1959	B. Stevens (Hemming)	1987	S. Symington
1929	K. Rowe	1960	B. Stevens (Hemming)	1988	S. Symington
1930	K. Rowe	1961	B. Stevens (Hemming)	1989	S. Symington
1931	K. Rowe	1962	B. Stevens (Hemming)	1990	T. Hoskin
1932	K. Rowe	1963	B. Stevens (Hemming)	1991	F. Symington
1932	K. Rowe	1964	C. Gately (King)	1992	D. Hemming
1933	K. Rowe	1965	P. Meehan	1993	A. Adlam
1934	K. Rowe	1966	P. Meehan	1994	C. Cawse
1935	K. Rowe	1967	P. Meehan	1995	D. Hemming
1936	K. Rowe	1968	P. Meehan	1996	A. Adlam
1937	K. Rowe	1969	L. Shepherd (Hughes)	1997	T. Hoskin
1938	K. Rowe	1970	L. Shepherd (Hughes)	1998	C. Cawse
1939	K. Rowe	1971	L. Shepherd (Hughes)	1999	T. Hoskin
1945	K. Rowe	1972	J. Yole (Leonard)	2000	T. Hoskin
1946	K. Rowe	1973	S. Tubb	2001	C. Cawse
1947	M. Moulton	1974	B. Hemming	2002	C. Cawse
1948	M. Moulton	1975	B. Hemming	2003	C. Cawse
1949	M. Moulton	1976	B. Hemming	2004	C. Cawse
1950	M. Moulton	1977	J. Leonard	2005	D. Hemming
1951	K. Rowe	1978	B. Hemming	2006	C. Cassidy
1952	J. Baker (Hockaday)	1979	J. Leonard	2007	A. Stitson
1953	P. Meehan	1980	J. Leonard	2008	C. Cassidy
1954	S. Bradley (Brook)	1981	B. Hemming	2009	A. Stitson

INDEX

113

BIBLIOGRAPHY

Admiralty Handbook. 1937. Manual of Seamanship Volume 1. His Majesty's Stationary Office, London. UK.

Aggett, Roger. A river of memories. Private publication.

Baring, Maurice. 2001. The puppet show of memory. House of Stratus. London. UK.

Farr, Grahame. 1968. Wreck and rescue on the coast of Devon. The story of the south Devon lifeboats. D. Bradford Barton Ltd., Truro. Cornwall. UK.

Private Nose. Various picks. Private publication.

South Devon Times. 26th August 1926.

Western Morning News. August 1954.

South Devon Times. 19th August 1983.

Yealm Regatta minutes book. 1933, 1964.

Yealm Regatta Programme. 1979, 1994, 1999.

C.1986 Launching Crabbers. Left to right D. Farleigh, T. Martin, P. Stitson, N. Shepherd, J. & P. leonard, S. Hockaday. P. Morrissey, L. Finch, H. Hockaday, S. Morrissey, N. Lethbridge, J. Shepherd. Photo courtesy of L. Matthias.